# UN CSW62 EMPOWERING WOMEN

## 50-50 BY 2030

## Dr. Veena Adige

# Notion Press

Old No. 38, New No. 6
McNichols Road, Chetpet
Chennai - 600 031

First Published by Notion Press 2018
Copyright © Veena Adige 2018
All Rights Reserved.

ISBN  978-1-64429-483-3

I dedicate this book to

My husband Mohandas Shenoy Adige

My children Priya-Rohit and Deepak-Sushma

My Grandchildren Shreya, Rithik and Arjun

CSW62
COMMISSION ON THE STATUS OF WOMEN

Reserved

# Contents


*Acknowledgments*.....................................................................vii

*Author's Note*.........................................................................ix

*United Nations (UN) and the Commision on
the Status of Women (CSW)* ............................................xiii

*Preface* .................................................................................xvii

1. Consultation Day and Opening Ceremony of CSW62...... 1

2. Interesting Seminars ............................................................ 9

3. Sessions ............................................................................... 17

4. Fifty Fifty by 2030............................................................. 45

5. Impressions of Delegates..................................................... 59

6. Benefits of Economic Empowerment of Women ............. 81

7. Some NGOs that participated in CSW62 ........................ 89

8. Indian Women speakers at CSW62 ................................. 111

9. Cultural Events .................................................................. 117

*Quotable Quotes*................................................................. 121

*Abbreviations and Stats*...................................................... 125

*Epilogue* ............................................................................. 127

# Acknowledgments

With deepest gratitude to

- Dame Dr Prof Meher Master-Moos, President of Zoroashtrian College, India
- Dr S. Giri Bhat
- Mrs Durga Shenoy
- United Nations
- Press releases from the UN CSW 62
- Delegates of UN CSW62

# Author's Note

While attending the United Nations CSW62 seminar in March 2018, I was impressed by the high level energy, the sincerity and the enthusiasm of women from all over the world. Each one of them had done some extraordinary work in her own country for which she had come to the United Nations to share, learn and follow. There were about four thousand four hundred women attending the four hundred odd events spread over two weeks in and around the United Nations. Each session was of one and a half hour duration with three to five women from different countries talking and answering questions from the dedicated audience. So much information was collected, processed and digested.

It set me thinking. There were press notes, suggestions, ideas, and requests from various NGOs regarding the empowerment of women. But this would reach the public only if these were circulated and made available to them. The seed for writing a book was born. I decided to collect information directly and through press releases, individuals whom I met and interacted and put them together in a book form for everyone to read and take action.

Empowering women who have been used to being docile, quiet, accepting a second grade treatment is no joke. It requires a lot of effort and thinking and planning. Which is what the UN Women are doing. As a journalist I found it important that I do my bit in spreading the word.

It was not easy. Mails were rarely answered. Request for permission were received by silence. And then my learned well-wishers said that since all were in the form of press releases, made for public consumption I could use them without fear. And there were tons of press releases which I collected and sorted.

I had taken hundreds of pictures and also collected some from photographer friends. I wrote to all those whom I had met during my UN visit and requested them to give their impressions of the CSW62. Some answered, with enthusiasm and pictures, others did not respond. I have collected a sizeable number of impressions and write ups from the delegates which I am using in this book.

It took me many days and weeks to sort out from the plethora of pages of press releases and articles. However I have managed to do so and here is the result. Should there be any discrepancies or wrong or misleading information, I apologize. They are not intentional.

I hope readers are able to follow the UN Women's ideas and dreams and hope this will be passed around to make Fifty fifty by Twenty thirty a viable dream. This book: UN CSW62: WOMEN EMPOWERMENT  gives my impressions and that of others during the CSW62 held in March 2018.

Dr Veena Adige, India
vadige@rediffmail.com

What could happen if women of
faith built each other up?
We are more powerful together
than divided.

BE YOURSELF
ACCEPT YOURSELF
VALUE YOURSELF
FORGIVE YOURSELF
BLESS YOURSELF
EXPRESS YOURSELF
TRUST YOURSELF
LOVE YOURSELF
EMPOWER YOURSELF
©LUPYTHA HERMIN

Partnership for
Effective Change
CSW62
Priority Theme:
Challenges and opportunities
in achieving gender equality
and the empowerment of
rural women and girls
March 12 - 23, 2018
United Nations Headquarters
New York City, NY

# United Nations (UN) and the Commision on the Status of Women (CSW)

The United Nations is an intergovernmental organization tasked to promote international co-operation and to create and maintain international order. It was founded on October 24, 1945, in San Francisco, CA with its Headquarters now in  New York City, NY.

The organization is financed by assessed and voluntary contributions from its member states. Its objectives include maintaining international peace and security, promoting human rights, fostering social and economic development, protecting the environment, and providing humanitarian aid in cases of famine, natural disaster, and armed conflict. The UN is the largest, most familiar, most internationally represented and most powerful intergovernmental organization in the world.

The UN has six principal organs: the General Assembly (the main deliberative assembly); the Security Council (for deciding certain resolutions for peace and security); the Economic and Social Council (ECOSOC; for promoting international economic and social co-operation and development); the Secretariat (for providing studies, information, and facilities needed by the UN); the International Court of Justice (the primary judicial organ); and the UN Trusteeship Council (inactive since 1994). UN System agencies include the World Bank Group, the World

Health Organization, the World Food Programme, UNESCO, and UNICEF. The UN's most prominent officer is the Secretary-General, an office held by Portuguese politician and diplomat António Guterres since 2017. Non-governmental organizations may be granted consultative status with ECOSOC and other agencies to participate in the UN's work.

The organization won the Nobel Peace Prize in 2001, and a number of its officers and agencies have also been awarded the prize.

There are 193 state members of the U.N. and two or three observers (Holy See, Palestine, and Taiwan). In addition to negotiations about war and peace, the U.N. runs social development and emergency relief programs.

Certain foundational documents frame all U.N. development programs. These are some of the principal ones – the Universal Declaration of Human Rights being the first and most basic. Almost all member states have ratified these declarations and conventions, intended to address the special concerns of women, children, indigenous people, and other vulnerable groups.

A big change occurred when the U.N. General Assembly agreed on a framework of 17 "Sustainable Development Goals" to guide social development planning up to 2030. Virtually *all* aid agencies, foundations, and non-governmental organizations use these as reference points in designing and justifying their programs.

These "SDGs" are quite specific. Each goal has an action plan spelled out in specific "targets." For example, SDG 4, to"Ensure inclusive and quality education for all and promote lifelong learning," has ten specific targets. One is to "eliminate gender disparities in education." Others are to "ensure equal access to education and vocational training for the vulnerable..." and to "substantially increase the supply of qualified teachers."

Creating these 17 goals and the 169 associated targets was a broadly inclusive process that went on for five years or more. By the time the SDG's were finalized, many thousands of people working in development world-wide had debated, discussed, and added to many drafts circulating widely among governmental and non-governmental agencies.

A unit called "U.N. Women" now does planning, research, and monitoring on issues of specific concern to women. Including women themselves and women's specific concerns in all aspects of social development is an important part of this agency's agenda.

The U.N. Commission on the Status of Women, first formed in 1947, is a functional commission of the Economic and Social Council, one of the principal organs of the U.N. It consists of governmental delegates from 45 states (selected geographically) at a time, serving four-year terms. There are five officers (Bureau Members).

The U.N. declared 1975 as "the year of the woman," and the following Decade of Women stimulated a lot of activity world-wide around women's human rights. Between 1975 and 1995 there were four world conferences of and for women.

In 1979 the U.N. General Assembly adopted the Convention on the Elimination of All Forms of Discrimination Against Women (CEDAW), and issued it for signature and ratification in 1981. CEDAW now has been ratified by almost all member states except a few.

At the last world conference on women (in Beijing in 1995) the U.N. issued the "Beijing Declaration and Platform for Action," an agreement among governments to actively promote women's rights. This is another foundational U.N. document. Every CSW meeting produces an "outcome document" summing up general principles.

Reality cannot match up to the very high aspirations expressed in these many conventions, declarations, plans, and promises. But they do serve as a beacon of hope to many small, isolated groups of women striving to improve their situations. And they provide a useful, common framework for everyone doing social development worldwide.

# Preface

## Speaking at the United Nations

**Speaking at the United Nations and presenting a paper is a great, grand, unforgettable experience. And that too, during the maiden entry as a delegate. Never in my wildest dreams did I envisage such an occurrence. I dream a lot, some of my dreams come true, others are just whiffs of air, disappearing within a short while. But this was too good. I still can't believe that I really went to the United Nations and gave a speech.**

When I visited the United States the first time, like any other tourist, I too went to the United Nations and was taken around and given all the details. I was impressed. Justifiably so since some top level conferences were going on and we could see the leaders of different countries speaking seriously but could not hear them.

The General Assembly hall looked so huge. I was told that it could seat around 1800 people comfortably. When I personally went there to see the Opening ceremony in March this year, it was full. Large, full of people, pin drop silence, except for the speakers, and very disciplined. Impressive. There was hardly any movement. Even the ushers who were controlling the crowds and giving entries to only pass holders were talking in hushed whispers or through sign language.

As tourists we had our pictures taken and converted into postage stamps which we gleefully sent to our near and dear ones. It was such an excitement to be able to visit the UN and get our faces on the stamps and actually use them. We shopped and bought souvenirs, even if expensive, were a relic of our visit there.

Not really satisfied, my husband and I went a second time a few visits later. Since my daughter and her family have settled in the US we go over often. And again I was impressed. I loved the flying flags, the tourist shopping centre, and even the security checks we were subjected to. It made the UN so very important.

When my grandson (my son's son) was born three years ago, I made a conscious decision to stay at home and look after him. I gave up my job as the Associate Editor of Bhavan's Journal and happily wrote articles, stories, books whenever time allowed, while looking after my delightful grandson. I was having a retired life, choosing to write if and when my mood allowed. Quiet, placid, enjoying looking after Arjun, my grandson.

Events took a different turn twenty months ago. The GSB Mahila shakha(Women's wing) in Mumbai, India, was celebrating their Diamond Jubilee and my name was proposed by the President, Durga Shenoy, for being awarded a Woman of Substance acknowledgement. This is awarded to women who have made a great impression in society by their work, their achievements. This was a great honour bestowed upon me for all the work I had done. I am a journalist and also a social worker. My husband and I are actively involved in looking after a self-aided English medium school in rural Panvel, near Mumbai in India. The school caters to seven villages around and we had started with just eight students which grew to four hundred and forty two, with the first batch appearing for the SSC Board exams in 2018(An important exam when children reach the Tenth grade). And the result is a cent per cent pass. A girl has stood first in the batch to our delight.

I also started a democratic Group called Vsisters (no office bearers, all members are equal) which has housewives from Navi Mumbai(a satellite town of Mumbai) meeting once in two months and having interesting and inventive programmes.

Vsisters was completing six years and had put together a hilarious Konkani language drama by six ladies who had absolutely no stage experience. The organisers of the Diamond Jubilee celebrations in Mumbai invited Vsisters to stage the drama and also honour me as a Woman of Substance. The huge hall was packed to capacity and when my bio data was presented, many in the audience were highly impressed.

I am a quiet type of a person rarely talking about myself. And I was in Nagpur, a city in Central India, for twenty four years where I was a popular figure before returning to Mumbai. I was the Assistant Editor of The Hitavada, the largest selling English newspaper in Vidarbha and Madhya Pradesh (States in Central India). I had also been instrumental in starting The Hitavada Twinkle Club which has twenty five thousand children as members. The Club is in the Limca Book of Records and could have been included in the Guinness Book of Records as there is no such club in the world which I discovered through emails and letters.

Also I hold a bachelor's degree in Science, another degree in Mass Communications and two Post graduate degrees in Public Administration and Linguistics. I have written four books and six ebooks, besides hundreds of articles, features, news items, stories, interviews and the like. My articles have been used as textbook material by the Maharashtra state SSC Board and several of my stories have been translated into various languages. All in all an impressive bio data.

There was one Dr S.G. Bhat in the audience that day, a friend who was also taken by surprise when my bio data was presented, since I did not enjoy as high a popularity in Mumbai as I had in Nagpur. After the program, he approached me and said that I was Ph.D material.

My husband had also been saying the same thing for years but I did not know how to go about it, and I wanted it in English literature but since I did not take English as my subject during my post-graduation, there was a very real doubt whether I would be accepted as a Ph.D student with English literature as my subject.

Dr Bhat said that there was another university, the Zoroastrian College in India which specialized in awarding Ph.D Degrees based on Research in different fields. I kept silent as I was busy looking after my grandson and had no time to run about, researching and writing.

He persisted and I contacted Dame Meher Master-Moos, the President of the Zoroashtrian College. When she saw my bio data she said that my Book, 'THE LEGACY OF BABA AMTE' published by Bharatiya Vidya Bhavan was a detailed research and I could get my doctorate based on that if I presented it in the standard format and did some more research.

To cut a long story short, I did exactly that and on June 3, 2017 I was the proud doctorate degree holder. Whether I was more delighted or whether my husband was delighted even more is debatable. But it was a great day. And a great achievement if I may say so. My daughter Priya came for a surprise three day visit from the US especially for the occasion and I was thrilled.

Dame Fortune had another surprise in store for me. When I was at Sanjan on the Maharashtra- Gujarat border (where the Zoroastrian College is based) while talking I mentioned Ram Krishnaa Academy, an English medium school  in rural Panvel where my husband and I are actively involved. Madam Moos immediately said that I should present a paper at the United Nations where the CSW62 had rural women and girls as its current theme. (The exact theme was "Challenges and Opportunities in achieving gender equality and empowerment of rural women and girls") It was right down my alley.

Madam sent my application as a delegate to the UN along with the names of six other ladies. By that time Madam had shifted from Mumbai to Sanjan where the internet connectivity was not very steady and she had great difficulty in getting through. Finally in December she could send our names before the deadline and we got an email in the affirmative. I was a delegate to the CSW62 (Commission on the Status of Women) and I was delighted. A chance of a lifetime. About five thousand women from over 150 countries of the world belonging to a thousand NGOs expected to participate in the fifteen day seminar (from March 12 to March 23, 2018) is an event to reckon with. And I was a chosen one, thanks to Madam Dame Meher Master-Moos, President of the Zoroastrian College and All India Behram Baug Society who had done all the ground work.

The main hurdle was crossed. Meanwhile I sent my bio data and other details to Laxmi Shah, the NGO's representative to the United Nations. After a suspenseful nail biting period I finally got the invitation from the Temple Of Understanding, another well-known NGO, to be on their panel and be a speaker! I was in the seventh heaven, jumping with joy, yet a bit nervous since ours was the very first session on March 12, 2018 at 8.30 a.m.!

My joy knew no bounds when I received this information on January 21 this year and I began my preparations in earnest. I spoke to the girl students of Rama Krishnaa Academy, their mothers, teachers, took pictures and googled all India status on the rural girl child. Armed with my papers I arrived at the United Nations, butterflies in my stomach but excited all the same. I got my ground pass and booked myself into a hotel. My daughter lives in Riverside Greenwich in Connecticut and I would have to have a long commute every day if I stayed with her.

Besides, I had landed in the eye of a snow storm and more were expected.

I got special permission for my daughter, son in law, children, and her friend to see and listen to me speaking. The Temple of Understanding which organized the event consisted of Alison Van

Dyk, and Grove Harris, two charming ladies and the speakers with me were Donna Bollinger, Executive Director, RPA, USA and Dr Angela Reed, RSM Coordinator, MIA: Mercy Global Action at the UN . I spoke for fifteen minutes about the rural girl child in India, about Rama Krishnaa Academy, the challenges and opportunities they have.

At the UN main buildings there were women, women everywhere, all cheerful, smiling and talking to each other. I noticed that the ladies who came to the United Nations are all great in their own fields and have no complexes. They are dedicated to whatever they do and speak freely about their work. There are no signs of ego or pride, all are sincere and dedicated.

I was all alone after the Opening ceremony as I did not know who else from India had come. I had met Dr Jayshree Borad from Bangalore the previous day and we had agreed to share the hotel room in New York. She had come and listened to my speech. But as she did not have a pass for the Opening Ceremony, she went to the hotel to deposit her luggage and then returned later.

The next day was wet with a bit of snow. Dr Jayshree and I took a cab and went to the main building for attending sessions. Here we met Dr Shivani Khetan from Delhi and we made a threesome, attending as many seminars as possible in the days that followed.

There were events at every two hour intervals. At the entrance of the reception in the main building there were huge timetables of the events. There were more than four hundred during the two week period. There were main events, parallel events and side events. There were also exhibitions, processions et al. There was so much to do and so much to attend. I was feeling a bit overwhelmed.

We had been given a handbook on all the events of NGO CSW62 during the Consultation Day on Sunday 11 March, 2018 at the Tribeca – Performing Arts Center Borough of Manhattan Community College (BMCC) and we went through it treating it like a holy Book. Each time slot had multiple events in different venues, some inside the UN Main Building and others around the building, either just across the street at the Church Centre or the UN Plaza or a few blocks away.

We chose which sessions we wanted to attend and kept a close tab on them. They all sounded interesting but due to the overwhelming number of sessions, we could pick and choose only a few.

**Grove Harris, Veena Adige, Laxmi Shah and Allison Van Dyk**

**Presenting a paper on Rural Girl Child: Opportunities and challenges. Also seen are Grove Harris, Donna Bollinger, and Dr Angela Reed**

# CHAPTER I
# Consultation Day and Opening Ceremony of CSW62

*We need a people-centered approach. Rural
women must be part of decision-making.*
— Phumzile Mlambo-Ngcuka,
UN Secretary General and Executive Director

The Consultation Day on Sunday March 11 was exciting, a preview of what was to come. Important names like Phumzile Mlambo-Ngcuka, Under-Secretary-General and Executive Director, UN Women, H.E. Ambassador Geraldine Byrne Nason, Permanent Representative Mission of Ireland; Bureau Chair, Commission on the Status of Women was on the invitation. Conversation was moderated by Lara Setrakian, of News Deeply.

The Keynote Address by the 2018 NGO CSW Woman of Distinction, Sizani Gubane, Founder of Rural Women's Movement, South Africa was juxtaposed with Panel Discussion- The Concerns of Rural Women- by Gia Gaspard Taylor, Network of Rural Women Producers, Trinidad and Tobago; Maria Luisa Mendonca, Network for Social Justice and Human Rights, Brazil; Lilly Be'Soer, Voice for Change, Jiwaka Province, New Guinea; Ruth Faircloth, Rural Migrant Ministry, New York State. The Moderator was Esther Mwaura, of GROOTS Kenya. It was a wonderful day long program, a curtain raiser to the two week seminar.

What a wonderful privilege it was to be a part of this great experience. I was representing Zoroashtrian College and All India Shah Behram Baug Society. Around 1000 UN Women from Nations across continents congregated at the TriBeCa Institute of Performing Arts, with one common goal in mind 'Achieving Gender Equality and empowering rural girls and women'. The whole atmosphere was fraught with emotion. 'Leave no one behind' was the resounding theme as speakers talked about encouraging, supporting and lifting women up as they climb the ladder.

After a welcome and introduction by Rosalee Keech & Jackie Witherspoon the session started with a colouful display of dancing from Mager Indigenous Youth dancers from Nepal. The first panel session was moderated by Lara Setrakian of News Deeply and Under Secretary General Phumzile Mlambo-Ngcuka and H.E. Ambassador Geraldine Byrne Nason outlined their hopes for the forthcoming sessions and expectations on the outcome documents.

Ngcuko emphasised that 'encouragement was the greatest gift one could give to women' and it was up to us to correct the trends that were going the wrong way. She said that farm workers who feed us go hungry and are invisible. There should be labour laws for domestic workers and those who work in agriculture. We should find answers for the policy failures in government. Byrne Nason stressed on the co-operation and power of NGO's to bring about awareness among rural women about the legal system and their land rights.

The 2018 woman of distinction, Sizani Ngubane founded the Rural Women's Movement South Africa. She gave an exceptional account of the abuse, inequality and struggles of the rural women as well as the successes they had achieved.

This was followed by a panel of representatives from across the globe including Trinidad and Tobago and Canada and all working in slightly different themes but all with rural women. Issues covered included violence against women, climate, land and property rights and migrant farm workers. After lunch four women in four countries through four different media told their stories.

This was followed by Convention on the Elimination of All Forms of Discrimination Against Women (CEDAW) awards to two American Mayors, one posthumously to Mayor Lee who was the inspiration of the first US CEDAW ordinance.

The session closed with the Lavender Light Gospel Chorus.

Dr Jayshreee and I went to the hotel to have a good night's sleep and to be fresh for the next day's program.

I met Grove Harris, Alison Van Dyk, Darcy Neill and others of the Temple of Understanding over coffee on March 12 at 8 in the morning and then we made our way to the Armenian Convention Centre for our session. I had obtained special permission for my daughter, son in law, children, and her friend to see and listen to me speaking. Grove Harris introduced us while Alison Van Dyke looked after the guests, saw to the recording and other matters. Laxmi Shah was present and so were many others whom I came to know later on. The other speakers were Donna Bollinger, Executive Director, RPA, USA and Dr Angela Reed RSM Coordinator, MIA: Mercy Global Action at the UN. I spoke extempore for fifteen minutes though I had my papers with me (and this, they said, came from my heart), pictures and recordings made and I was happy and satisfied at the accolades heaped upon me.

I had to rush for the Opening Ceremony in the UN of CSW62 which was at 10 a.m. and I had received a pass (each NGO was given one pass each as there were so many organizations that had sent delegates and everyone could not be accommodated). My daughter dropped me at the main building entrance and I rushed to the fourth floor where I could see the Opening Ceremony from the balcony. I pinched myself to see whether I was dreaming or was I really in the United Nations, having given my presentation and was now watching the Opening Ceremony live. It was very impressive. So many ladies from so many countries, the UN office bearers, and several big personalities were all there. I was busy clicking and looking around to listen to the proceedings.

Geraldine Byrne Nason (Ireland), Chair of the sixty-second session of the Commission on the Status of Women, welcomed all participants, especially those civil society representatives whose engagement would ensure the Commission's work took a tangible form in communities across the globe. Urging all participants to deliver concrete, actionable results, she said the Commission should not be known as a meeting or an acronym, but as an instrument to truly promote the rights of women around the globe. "We have a moral obligation as we begin our work," she stressed, calling on the Commission to "do more and do better". Participants must be honest in recognizing shortcomings that had long impeded the progress of women and girls, and strive harder to reach the goals enshrined in the of 1995 Beijing Platform for Action.

Also welcoming this session's focus on the rights and empowerment of rural women and girls, she recalled that women in her native Ireland — one of the most rural of all the countries in Europe — knew what it meant to struggle against such challenges as food shortages, poverty and migration. However, Irish women had become unrivalled agents of change, helping their country develop rapidly. While data today revealed that women and girls still suffered disproportionately from global challenges, they also led the fight to end hunger and poverty, shine light on injustice and build peace in local communities around the world. Rural women and girls must be at the heart of the United Nations sustainable development efforts, she stressed, urging the Organization to redouble efforts to bring them to the decision-making table. Calling, in particular, for normative guidance, action-oriented commitments and tangible results on the part of policy makers, she described the current session as a key moment on the path to ending discrimination against women and girls once and for all. Indeed, she concluded, "time is up" on women taking second place around the world.

Antonio Gutterres, Secretary-General of the United Nations, said that women around the world were telling their stories, from "#MeToo" to "#TimesUp", calling out abusive behaviour and discrimination. Centuries of patriarchy had left a damaging legacy, with women underrepresented in science, art and at the United Nations, where female ambassadors hovered around 20 per cent. "It is only when we have changed statistics like these that we can truly say we are in a new era for women and girls," he said. "By building equality, we give women a chance to fulfill their potential. We also build more stable societies."

The Commission's theme focusing on rural women addressed a marginalized group, he said. They were often the backbone of their families and communities, managing land and resources. The Commission was leading the way to listen to and support them. Doing so was essential to fulfilling the 2030 Agenda for Sustainable Development. Highlighting some of the steps the United Nations had taken since he became Secretary-General, he said gender parity in the Senior Management Group had been met for the first time. A zero-tolerance policy on sexual harassment had been established and an initiative was addressing sexual exploitation and abuse by those serving the United Nations.

Marie Chatardova (Czech Republic), President of the Economic and Social Council, said the Commission was a critical instrument in the United Nations efforts to strengthen the global normative framework for the empowerment of women and the promotion of gender equality. Noting that it was also a key driver of the Economic and Social Council's work, she said the Commission's outcomes would help support the 2030 Agenda's implementation, as well as that of its 17 Sustainable Development Goals. During its forthcoming session, the High-Level Political Forum under the Council's auspices would consider the theme, "Transformation towards Sustainable and Resilient Societies", focusing on Goal 6 on water and sanitation, Goal 7 on energy for all, Goal 11 on cities and human settlements, Goal 12 on sustainable consumption and production, Goal 15 on life on earth and Goal 17 on partnerships.

Phumzile Mlambo-Ngcuka, Under-Secretary-General for Gender Equality and Executive Director of the United Nations Entity for Gender Equality and the Empowerment of Women (UN-Women) said women in rural areas were lagging in every gender and development indicator. Moreover, progress was slowing and even reversing. "It has never been so urgent to hold leaders accountable for their promises for accelerating progress" on the Sustainable Development Goals, she said. An unprecedented hunger for change in women's lives was being seen around the world, as well as a growing recognition that when women banded together, "they can make demands that bite".

I had also obtained a pass for the Round Table Conference and I was impressed by the people who had come from so many countries. The topic was 'Good practices in the empowerment of rural women and girls, including through prevention of gender-based violence and through access to justice, social services and health care'. There were so many important ministers and I heard the Ministers from Costa Rica, Australia, Egypt, Paraguay, Norway, Saudi Arabia and other places speaking. I was busy craning my neck to see them. Their discussions were not very clear to me, but the very fact that I was in such high society, seeped into me and I again pinched myself to see whether it was real or a dream.

This session was chaired by by Indrk Saar, Minister for Culture of Estonia and Margaret Kobla, Cabinet Secretary for Public Service, Youth and Gender Affairs of Kenya.

Mr. Saar, said that realizing the right of rural women and girls to quality, affordable and accessible education was not only at the core of Goal 4, but also a stepping stone for economic empowerment, political participation and the exercise of many other rights. He asked Ministers participating in the discussion to highlight steps being taken by their Governments to ensure affordable quality education for rural women and girls; what investments they were making to ensure that sustainable energy, transport, water and sanitation improved the lives of rural women and girls; initiatives undertaken by Member States to ensure that information and communications technologies benefited rural women and girls; and national policies that helped rural women and girls gain access to quality food and nutrition.

The Minister for Women of Australia, who also held the portfolio of Minister for Revenue and Financial Service, said national broadband and mobile "black spot" networks were being rolled out in her country with the aim of closing the digital gap in rural areas. Meanwhile, a national plan to combat violence against women and girls would ensure that those in rural areas would have access to the same level of support as their urban counterparts.

**With Inputs from: Barbara Dixon: Rayna Rees, Daphne Pillai and press releases**

## Consultation day

# Chapter II
# Interesting Seminars

*Women don't always know how strong they are.*
— Anastasia Mikova, film maker

As the days continued we made more friends and acquaintances, exchanged visiting cards and information and vague promises of keeping in touch.

Besides attending as many events as we could, we focused on getting to know other delegates, eagerly learning about them and their work. It was fascinating to see how much work was being done for women, especially the rural ones (as this was the theme).

We saw the First Lady of Nigeria, Queen Mother of Africa and other luminaries from other countries, ministers from all over the world, social workers, women of faith and others and they were all so polite and nice. During the seminars, presentations and discussions, there was pin drop silence. No cell rings, no coughs or sneezes either. And all listened attentively. But in the various cafeterias, there were women talking animatedly or sitting quietly, some clicking pics while others eating hungrily. Here we met several interesting people. Charging of mobile phones was the meeting point for several delegates.

I met a couple of beautiful and enthusiastic Brazilian girls in the cafe and they invited me and my friends to their event. We attended the event and the girls were so thrilled! Though their discussions were in Spanish and Portuguese, there were translators and we had no problem. Ninety five per cent speeches and discussions I attended at the UN were in English.

Being at the United Nations is a great experience. The women from all over the world came together to discuss about the rural women, their problems, their challenges. Women dressed in colourful attire rubbed shoulders with the black and white dresses of the local people, the bonhomie exhibited by all was something one has to see and experience. There was no discrimination, instant friendships were made and there was laughter in the cafes and pin drop silence during the sessions. All speeches were listened with great interest, questions asked and answered.

The problems women face are the same worldwide, in different formats. Child marriages, trafficking, domestic violence, gender discrimination, patriarchal society are all similar the world over, I felt as I listened to a few discussions. These women who have come are representatives of their countries, the educated cream of society. Each one is an important person with an interesting story of her own.

I met ladies from New Zealand, Kenya, Japan, Pakistan, Bangladesh, Nepal, Peru, Ecuador, Canada, Brazil, Nigeria, Ghana, UK, and many others. All were eager to talk and exchange notes. My colourful silk saris (Madam Moos had insisted that I wear saris as a proud Indian) were instant hits and people took pics of me while others eyed me with interest. During the seminar I noticed that India held an important place. There were references to India and Indians, and there were a few Indian speakers like Dr. Pam Rajput of Delhi.

At the LaQuinta hotel where we stayed, a woman from Africa in the breakfast room greeted me with a Namaste (Indian form of greeting with folded hands). She began speaking in Hindi, an Indian language (yes, Hindi) and told me, 'Mera pehla bachcha Pune mein hua tha (My first child was born in Pune). Pune is two hours drive from Mumbai. She and her husband were studying in Pune where she had learnt Hindi. I was impressed.

Dr Shivani Khetan from Delhi, Dr Jayshree Borad from Bangalore, a couple of girls from Nepal and Bangladesh and a photographer from Florida became good friends. Because of the large number of women, the conference rooms would get filled up fast and there was not even standing space in some. Delegates sitting on the floor and making notes was quite a normal procedure.

Each session focused on a different aspect of rural girls and women simultaneously and we would go to the ones which caught our interest. We made notes, listened, asked questions. And we met interesting people like the Queen Mother Dr. Delois N. Blakely, who had come to the United Nations seminars for the forty ninth time!!

Dr. Blakely, who is 61 years old, dresses in a colorful African style, and has been a mayor of Harlem for the last eight years. She has headquarters in an ordinary-looking apartment house on West 142nd Street in New York, although her true office is Harlem itself, which she traverses each day on foot from 6 a.m. until after dark at a pace that is faster and perhaps more reckless than most of the New York's yellow cabs.

"I have what you might call a traveling office," she said "I am a 24/7 operation. There is no such thing as 9 to 5 when you are servicing the community." In that service, Ms. Blakely does anything from approaching a state senator, petitioning City Hall or speaking with police officers at the local station house. For this she receives no payment other than the gratitude of her constituents. She has received her master's degree from Harvard and a doctorate in education from Columbia.

Interestingly she had no visiting card. We took pics of the only one she had. She did not need one as she was so well known as we could see from the way people flocked to her. She spoke well, had interesting comments to make.

During the fifteen days I met several others also and had invigorating talks with them. Dr Sarah Turner, a Professor from Canada who hailed from New Zealand and we had many things to discus. She spoke of rural Canada and rural New Zealand and the problems they had were similar to those the world over.

I met another New Zealander whose father is from Kerala, a state in South India and she was thrilled to talk about her country and mine. The ladies from Bangla Desh, Pakistan and Nepal recognized each other and we made an interesting group.

Town Hall meeting with Secretary General & Civil Society was a full house with not a single chair vacant and it was one of the most sought after events. We could not attend it though we had confirmed invitations and had to get this information second hand.

The Under-Secretary General and Executive Director of UN Women Dr. Phumzile Mlambo-Ngcuk, a very down to earth lady walked in with the Secretary General (SG) Antonio Guterres and their entourage in the midst of cheering from the audience.

The huge conference hall was vibrant and everyone was eager to hear the Secretary General. As per Article 97 of the UN Charter, the SG is the "Chief Administrative Officer" of UN in all meetings of the General Assembly, the Security Council, Economic and Social Council and Trusteeship Council, he performs such functions as these organs entrust upon him, so he is really the head of the UN in the true sense of the word.

SG began on a confident note by saying that "it is a male dominated world and the question is that of power. Power usually is not given but taken, so conditions have to be made to give the power and over years and by such events such conditions are made for easy transfer of power". These words made everyone at ease and eager to hear him, he talked about the gender balance in the UN workforce; he said that a few years earlier in the

Executive office the ratio was 60% men and 40% women. Now it is 56% of women and 44% of men, exhibiting his seriousness in this business.

He proceeded to address three important issues, first about his mandate to bring in full parity by 2028 for which he said nearly 88% of the departments had set their road maps for the same.

Second, is to put in place zero tolerance on sexual exploitation within the organisation, he expressed concerns in areas of resettlement of people, refugee camps and sexual violence by soldiers.

Third he spoke about elimination of sexual harassment in the work place i.e. the UN itself, 50 complaints of sexual harassment during the last year was quite alarming and so he said that strict measures are being taken to provide help lines for staff to express their difficulties confidentially, he spoke about setting up of specialized security unit which will investigate these issues only.

**Inputs from delegates and press releases**

**Dr Veena Adige, Dr Jayshree Borad and Dr Shivani Ketan with delegates from Nepal**

**With African Queen Mother**

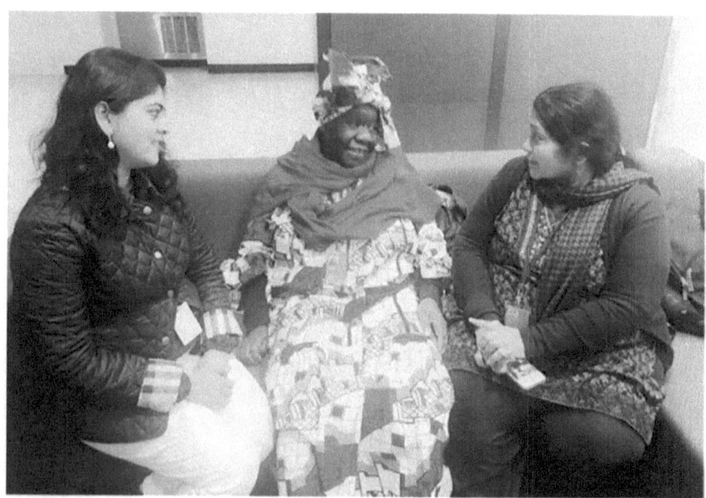

## With Brazilian delegates

# Chapter III
# Sessions

*We rural women need to stand up and say, "We are somebody."
Women coming together here and all speaking together have a
powerful voice. Let's not just talk about it. Let's do it.*
　　　　　　　　　　　– Ruth Faircloth, Rural Migrant Ministry

There were Sessions in the main building, parallel and side events in places around the United Nations. Salvation army, The Armenian Convention centre, Fifth Avenue, Church Centre, were some of the avenues. They were not far away from each other. But there were so many events that to go from one event to the other took time and some got filled up so fast that we did not have any entry, though we had informed them in advance. Long queues would be formed half an hour before the session. There was a short gap between two events so though it was possible to attend many, time was the culprit and we had to skip some we really wanted to attend.

The Opening Session was on the first day at 10 a.m at the UN Headquarters General Assembly. The Chair for CSW62 was announced formally- Ambassador to Republic of Ireland Her Excellency Geraldine Byrne Nasson followed by the other Commission positions.

Although so many people fight to get into the Opening Session as it is seen as significant, most of the business is not contentious since it is mainly covering the formalities of the governance of the work for the next two weeks. One of the most important appointments after the Chair is that of facilitator for the negotiations on the Agreed Conclusions. As with most of this work for this session, agreements have been reached in advance and the confirmations are formalities, including the agenda and rules for the way in which the Commission will conduct its business.

Many important people including the new Chair, the UN Secretary General and the Executive Director of UN Women, Phumzile Mlambo-Ngcuka, made opening statements in support of the work of the Commission. The session delivered many memorable quotes from all the speakers, including: "We need agreed conclusions and agreements – had enough rhetoric", "The time is opportune, we will no longer take second place", "The central question is power – it needs to be given not taken" and "We know the meaning of women's rights – we just need them". There were dozens of contributions from around the globe, all asserting their commitment to the progress of women and to the achievement of SDG #5.

My talk was at the Armenian Convention centre on Monday March 12 at 8.30 a.m. Sponsored by  the Temple of Understanding it began with Grove Harris introducing the topic and the speakers. Then each one of us spoke on our topic for about fifteen minutes each and then there were questions and answers. Since my topic was on rural girl child's education and challenges, one of the questions aimed at me was on connectivity in rural areas. It seemed this was a problem in many countries of the world. With everyone going technical, and computer and internet savvy, the expectation is that connectivity is available in all corners of the world. But this is not so. Even in the progressive countries there are connectivity problems.

Along with my session, there were sessions on role on media in promoting, women's rights to freedom of religion and expression, Using technology and innovation to bridge the rural/ urban digital gap, eco village movement pioneering sustainable livelihoods and others at various venues at the same time. On an average there were about ten to eleven events at each time slot.

So one can imagine the number of programs a sincere delegate could attend. Each conference room in the UN main building, on an average had a seating capacity of about a hundred delegates, fully equipped with speaker phones, sometimes computers, and other necessities. The four to six speakers would be seated in the centre with delegates in front, back and sides. The format was similar. The moderator would introduce the subject and the speakers and each one was allotted ten to fifteen minutes and this would be followed by a question answer session. The panel of speakers generally was from different countries. Thus there would be Caucasians, Africans, Asians and others presenting through a common platform.

We were very keen on attending the event from India and took special pains to reach on time. I would have liked to give a presentation there but it was too late as the speakers and timings were finalized. The Ministry of Woman and Child Development, India, presented the topic 'Challenges and opportunities in achieving gender equality and the empowerment of rural women and girls' in the Conference room 12 of the main General Assembly room. Paulomi Tripathi, First Secretary, Permanent Mission of India to the UN, and Subbalaxmi were the coordinators. It was an interesting seminar with Dr Nandini Azad, Chairperson of The Independent Commission for People's Rights and Development, New Delhi; President ,India Co-operative Network for Women Limited, Board Member of National Women's Credit Fund , Acting Chairperson, Women's Committee International Co-operative Alliance, Asia-Pacific and many others stepping in with her views. The discussion was that the mindset of the patriarchal society in India was taking a long time to change. And that India is moving from women's development to women led development.

Highlights of the projects were setting up of One Stop Centres for helping women in distress to address all the different kind of issues and difficulties faced by women, these centres are equipped in such a way that all kinds of problems suffered by rural women would be addressed. These centers were to be set up in close proximity to police stations and hospitals to facilitate easy access to these requirements. The centers would also provide counselling and legal aid services. New custom made buildings were being built to cater to this unique need of the project under one roof. Another project provided for financial assistance to pregnant and lactating women which though was an ongoing project, there were no statistic projected about its reach.

One project was providing loan to women entrepreneurs, another which required a mention was providing training to elected women representatives about their roles and encourage them to actually sit in their positions and participate in the development process. It was a well organized session.

A Dialogue and meditation with Her Holiness Amma Sri Karunamayi was held at the Salvation Army hall on March 13 at 8.30 in the morning. People were fascinated by her.

'The Last Girl and her vulnerabilities to sex trafficking ' was sponsored by Apne Aap Women Worldwide and had Ruchira Gupta, Founder President of Apne Aap; Cynthia Stephen, Policy Researcher working with the Dalit Community; Mickey Meji, Survivor Activist, Embrace Dignity, South Africa and Rebecca Bender, Survivor Leader and Shanta Roy, Survivor Activist from Canada giving their views.

We had met the Queen Mother several times and when we found out that there was a high level side event at the United Nations Church Centre on March 15 , we reached by 8.30 a.m.

Queen Mother Dr Deloise Blakely gave the welcome speech. The topic was the 2030 agenda-Economic and Educational Advancement of Women and Girls. H E Martha Udom, the wife of the Governor of Akwa Ibom state of Nigeria was the main speaker who outlined the happenings in Nigeria. Other speakers were from Mali, France, Mauritania and United States.

'Transforming society through Empowerment of Rural Women' was the theme of the session at the United Headquarters Conference Room 11 room on March 16. Though the other speakers were good we were impressed by Dr Pam Rajput of Delhi University who spoke with passion and force. She declared that 'Women are not invitees to this planet, we belong here. Women are necessary for success. Villages are roots of a nation. Women have strong roots. We can build a nation'.

In another session, the speaker Ruchira Gupta, a journalist from New York University drew a connection between porn and sex violence. She spoke forcefully saying that women go to great lengths to include even reconstruction of their vaginas to tow down to men's preferences! The new ones are the ultimate in beauty and are status symbols!!! Pepsie from Nigeria declared that men are not sexually appealing hence they use beautiful girls as cheerleaders during sports matches. She said that rape is a crime of power rather than that of desire. A documentary 'Selling of Innocence' was screened on the occasion.

Digital and Financial solutions were discussed by a panel at the Hilton Hotel, UN Plaza on March 20. The talk was on Contacts, targets, reactions, education, learning internet, financial literacy, loans etc.

Pulitzer Prize winner journalist Mr Matthew Garuana Galizia addressed the session on 'Safe Journalists, strong democracies' at the UN headquarters organized by the UNESCO panel. The safety of women journalists has become one of the most important issues for journalists in this digital era. Women journalists can be placed in vulnerable settings, at workplace and in the field and online, making them open to all kinds of harassment, intimidation and sometimes even violence. The panelists gave their first hand experiences of threats and consequences. Ms Alison Smale, Under-Secretary–General for Global Communications, Department of Public Information, UN; Mr Guy Berger, Director of Freedom of Expression and Media Development, UNESCO, Ms Maria Ressa, CEO and Executive Director of Rappler, Ms Jennifer Clement, President of PEN International. Ms Abeer Sa'ady, Vice President of International Association of Women in Radio and Television were the other speakers who shared their experiences.

'Empowering Rural Women' organized by the Temple of Understanding, a Non-Governmental Organization (NGO) in Consultative Status with the UN Economic and Social Council, is an active member of the NGO community working on the inside of the United Nations to advance social justice. The TOU actively supports the aims and principles of the United Nations by attending world summit meetings, sponsoring programs for NGOs, and participating on committees and coalitions of NGOs with similar values. Donna Bollinger, Executive Director, RFP-USA; Veena Adige, Advocate for Education for Rural Girls, India and Angela Reed, RSM Coordinator, Mercy International Association: Mercy Global Action at the UN were the speakers. Grove Harris was the Moderator and respondent of the Temple of Understanding. Donna Bollinger who has worked in 25 countries spoke about her work while Veena Adige spoke of the rural girl child in India and her education. Angela Reed spoke about human trafficking in the Phillipines.

Through the Zonta programme girls and women learn skills to make them independent. The Ambassador for Nepal stated that Nepal is a microcosm of the world, a melting pot where women are honoured and worshiped. He said that amazing progress had been made since the 1950s and women have played a large part in this. 30- 40% of government ministers are women.

The consul general said the aim is to make women powerful through education and employment but that resources are needed for training. Women are becoming more aware of their rights and robust structures are in place for inclusion of women in government roles. Women are inspired to do things for themselves. The session ended with the ambassador admitting that there was still a long way to go to achieve their aims and to reach the rural areas where women and girls are more vulnerable to early marriage and poverty.

SDG 5 recognises that trafficking is a violation of human rights and gender based violence, which is usually gender specific and is a violation of human rights. 71% of those trafficked are women and girls. Survivors of trafficking gave very moving accounts of their experiences explaining that victims see themselves as worthless and are often women of colour purchased by white, privileged men. Actor Mira Sorvino suggested a link between pornography and violence. She agreed that demand goes down when users are blamed. The conclusion was that sex trafficking and prostitution is a distinct crime and not part of modern day slavery.

Daphne Pillai, Founder President SI-Bombay-Chembur presented the challenges faced by rural women and girls in India with case study references to successful Soroptimist projects in her region of Mumbai- India. These initiatives have been meeting the very real needs of the women and were identified through participatory consultations and evidence based need assessments. The top priorities requested by these rural women and girls were support to improve their spoken English skills and development of practical skills which would enable them to generate independent income. These community level grassroots interventions are great examples of Soroptimists' aims: educating, enabling and empowering "in action" and were contrasted by Dr Pillai with what can often be rhetoric in the plethora of government regulations which are passed though not often implemented as evidenced by the C&AG's independent report.

Sr Annie Jesus Mary Louis from India spoke on 'Prostitution as violence against rural women'. She works to rescue and rehabilitate trafficked girls in the region of Chattisgarh. Young rural girls are lured by traffickers who appear in the guise of benevolent godfathers. If education is provided to the girls, this evil could be choked. She said if there was no supply then the demand would also dry up. Her appeal was to support organizations working against human trafficking in rural areas.

Anuradha Pradeep, President SI-Bangalore spoke on 'Empowerment of Women living in rural areas and Government support'. Rural women need support in two categories which she identified as 1) Physical which would include nutrition, menstruation, pregnancy, sexual and old age and 2) Psychological issues like providing them with life skills like communication skills, cultivating positive attitude, capacity to face difficult situations, counseling, etc. She emphasized the importance of government support in aiding rural women. The government has the power to make the policies, to control, to provide the infrastructure and the authority to implement. However, she cautioned that in developing and under developed countries due to corruption and indifferent attitudes, it is best to be careful before seeking government support.

Other speakers were Dr Sylvia Walker from Trinidad and Tobago whose topic was "Education Rural Women: Real Life." and Poppy Ullett who spoke on "Political participation for rural women."

The session successfully brought out the challenges of addressing the needs of rural women in different countries and the various interventions and best practices that have been undertaken to tackle these issues. The session also offered solutions and pathways to address the problems of rural women.

'Empowering girls everywhere: Pathways to end violence against children' is a major global issue and affects children in all societies and countries. In this panel discussion Arelys Bellorini of 'World Vision' was in the chair. She said that violence against children came in many forms like child marriage, female genital mutilation, sex trafficking and others.

Seated on the dais with the adult panelists was a little girl named Xhorda from Albania. She was one of the panelists in the forum. She was around 12 years old, a young leader advocating for children's participation on forums which speak about children's rights. She has been campaigning on children's issues and was disappointed that their voice is not taken seriously by the policy makers. Xhorda strongly felt that if you are talking about children, the children should have every right to relate their stories from their points of view.

Justice Joana from the Supreme Court of Mozambique stated that child marriage in Mozambique happened largely due to poverty and traditional culture. Children who resist this practice have no one to turn to. In rural cultures it is difficult to reach the judiciary. The government of Mozambique has tried to find a pathway to address this issue by introducing mobile tribunals to go to remote areas. These mobile tribunals create awareness and spread information about the illegality of forcing children into early marriages and other scourges that afflict children.

Manus de Barra represented the United Nations Office of the Special Representative of the Secretary General (OSRSG) which works towards ending violence against children.

The organisation advocates that children should have the right to participate in decisions that affect them. Child helpline mechanisms hardly exist and even if they do children are petrified to tell their stories for fear of repercussions. Staff employed in children helplines should be very sensitive when they receive an SOS from a child and the privacy and the confidentiality of the caller should be respected. There should also be prompt follow-up action and legal aid should be provided to the children who have appealed for help. Children will only voice their stories if they know that there are strong child protection policies to safeguard them from further violence.

Debra Jones from 'Save the Children' Foundation spoke on violence against children affected by armed conflict. She was counselling a child refugee from Syria. When Debra asked the kid what she would like on Valentine's Day, the reply was that the Valentine heart should be painted red as a symbol to end bloodshed. It is a protracted crisis for children in armed conflict. There is lack of pathways open to rehabilitate children during conflict and post conflict for recovery and rebuilding their lives. Her organisation practised 'mental health healing arts' for children who undergo trauma.

Diana Quick from the 'Child Fund Alliance' said that their organisation's central goal is to work with children, their rights and to provide a child protection system to ensure their safety.

Little Xhorda made a great impact. In the Question/ Answer session, most of the questions were directed at her and she was confidently able to reply to them all. The message powerfully went through. If a law is being framed for children, then children's voices should be the dominant voice in the discussions and in the policy making. 'NOTHING ABOUT US WITHOUT US'

'Child marriage, prostitution, trafficking and widows': all subjects that SIGBI are working on, so it was interesting to go to events which covered these subjects to see how other countries are handling the issues. The first session on prostitution and trafficking was very emotional as we heard testimonies from 4 victims. Their stories had the whole audience in tears and the Moderator Einar Gunnarsson stated he felt ashamed to be a man when he heard what the women had suffered.

Civil society was urged to lobby for the implementation of the Nordic model and for funding and education so that vulnerable women are not compelled to sell their bodies to feed themselves or their families.

Zambia and Malawi co-hosted a session on ending child marriage and outlined the strategies they had used to reduce the statistics in their own countries. Both countries were fortunate to have supportive male Presidents who collaborated on legislation to reduce child marriage. The biggest cause was poverty and lack of education. Many child marriages are now being annulled and social cash funding is being provided so that the girls can support themselves and can re- enter the education system. Cash advances were also being made available for special needs children and for those having suffered fistulae as a result of obstructed pregnancy.

The session on widows highlighted how girls can become serial widows. Married at a young age to men much older they can be widowed whilst still in their teens. They are then remarried and the system starts again.

In parts of Africa where there is conflict a girl may be a child bride, her husband is murdered by insurgents- she is then taken as a bride for the soldiers. Her soldier husband may be killed in the next conflict and the cycle starts again. These girls are often passed around as soldier brides and have children. If and when

they return home they are ostracised as they have "bad blood".

'Ignite the light' – UK and Northern Island: Across the globe, there are 130 million girls out of school. In Nigeria there have been Budget cuts and there are many barriers to girls' education. Girls drop out due to lack of funds and there is a fear of kidnapping in rural areas. Investment means a better world.

Penny Mordaunt MP stated that they have a 12-year commitment that by 2030 all girls will be in school. It was agreed that they must invest in good teaching, better schools and a commitment to STEM subjects. Education changes lives; it is the ladder out of poverty. Rural girls are susceptible to lack of education, early marriage, chores etc. We need quality education…good teachers, good pay to give children the tools they need for a better life or we will lose half the potential for progress. The session agreed that schools reflect wider society and can act as agents of change helping to reform practices of boys as leaders.

The topic was a very challenging one – 'Internet Generation as Pioneer: Rural Women's Opportunities and Challenges.' The speakers were from Taiwan, Canada, Nigeria and France. What we heard were huge eye openers. While Taiwan was using the Internet as a tool in rural areas to bridge the gap between rural and urban, the speaker from Canada regretfully said that even though Canada is a developed country, internet services had either not reached the rural areas or they were unaffordable. She was shocked when she saw advertisements in New York where cell phones and data plans were available for just $29 a month. She emphasised that in a digital economy, cell phones are important specially for those living at risk, but issues that rural women face are hidden and invisible making it difficult to advocate for them.

We had a lot of lessons to learn through the story of a rural Taiwanese girl named Shen-Xing-Ling. Before the internet age, she and her family had to be at the morning market at 4 am, and then it was the evening market which continued till night. Most of her sleep was in the truck that carried the agriculture products. But when she had access to the internet, she started selling crops through email and was thrilled that buyers for her 'pomelos' were just a click away.

The Kenya speaker described our current age as Generation Z. The generation of Facebook, Twitter, Google and other social media fixations for the youth. It is an age when a mother has to convince her child that 'I didn't download you. I gave birth to you.' The representative from Nigeria spoke on the 'Kids of the Past versus the Internet Generation.' Today digital technology dominates their lives. The final speaker was from France who felt that the internet was a curse as it has become a medium for human trafficking. She had some spine chilling facts to share about internet advertisements that sell a girl child.

The session gave plenty of insights into the different challenges faced by different countries in using the Internet.

Malawi's participation at the CSW62 was led by Minister of Gender, Children, Disability and Social Welfare Jean Kalilani. The minister told the commission that Malawi has reduced child marriages from 50 percent in 2015 to 42 out of 100 in 2017.

"In Malawi, over 50 percent of women aged between 20 to 24 years were married before the age of 18 between 2015 and

2016. About four percent of the population was married below the age of 15 while 24 percent was married before 18," she said.

"However, the investments in ending the vice have reduced the prevalence rate from 50 percent in 2015 to 42 percent in 2017. More girls are now going to school in the country because of strong efforts to end child marriages."

Kalilani touted the harmonisation of the marriage law, the amendment of the country's Constitution to increase the marriage age to 18 years, the introduction of chief's by-laws that seek to end child marriages and the 2017 National Strategy on ending Child Marriages as some of the reforms that have led to the achievement.

In February this year, Kalilani told the Rural Women Conference in Dowa that systemic inequalities and discriminatory practices against women still persist.

"These barriers prevent women from breaking the vicious cycle of poverty to fully enjoy their human rights and contribute meaningfully to the achievement of the SDGs," she lamented.

Kalilani said notable areas of discrimination are in economic empowerment, education, gender-based violence, health and well-being, among others.

The minister's concern is well etched in UN Women's Global Data-base on violence against women, which puts the prevalence of physical or sexual intimate partner violence at 34 percent in the country.

To tame the tide, ActionAid Malawi, one of the civil society organisations that attended the CSW 62, reckons that it is now time to empower grass-roots based women-led organisations to challenge and shift patriarchal socially constructed norms, practices or systems that facilitate and rationalise violence against women and girls including, systematic denial of access and control of productive resources.

"There is also need for coordinated efforts to address structural barriers that limit women's political participation and representation in leadership and decision-making positions," says ActionAid Malawi executive director Grace Malera.

Malera's remarks resonate well with the commission's resolution that emphasises the mutually reinforcing relationship on achieving gender equality and the empowerment of all women and girls, including those in rural areas. The commission further acknowledges that gender equality and the empowerment of rural women and girls and women's full and equal participation and leadership in the economy are essential for achieving sustainable development, promoting peaceful, just and inclusive societies, enhancing sustained, inclusive and sustainable economic growth and productivity.

# UN CSW62: Through Suzanne Hanchett's eyes

(Suzanne Hanchett, Partner, Planning Alternatives for Change, LLC Vice President, International Women's Anthropology Conference, is a social anthropologist with a doctorate from Columbia University. She is a Partner in the consulting firm, Planning Alternatives for Change LLC and a Researcher associated with the Center for Political Ecology. Her **Books:** Water Culture in South Asia: Bangladesh Perspectives, Coloured Rice: Symbolic Structure in Hindu Family Festivals. She did her first anthropological fieldwork in Karnataka (called Mysore State at that time)

UN Women and the Commission on the Status of Women have a definite agenda. They focus on certain priority issues within each year's theme.

A constant focus is girls' education. A touching video at this year's inaugural session featured a young girl in India skipping home from her village school as she proudly announced to everyone she met, that she would pass her exams, get promoted, and have a career of her own some day. The adults she encountered discouraged her. They told her that she was destined to marry at a young age, that education was not for girls, and so on. By the time she got home, she was miserable and dejected. When she saw her father, she accused him of lying to her about the importance of going to school. Her father reassured her that she would reach her goals. And she did. The closing message was: wait until girls are past 18 before getting them married.

Another, subliminal message was: men are an important part of the change that girls need. Another film was about an Iranian girl who wanted to be an astronaut. She had her own telescope. Her father had died, and her uncle was the head of the family. He threatened her, saying that he would definitely kill her if she did "anything wrong" while pursuing her educational goals.

People come to this conference for different reasons. Everyone enjoys an international trip, though it was very cold and snowing this year, and women from tropical countries didn't all have warm clothing. Many governments and "NGO's" come to showcase their achievements. One session on agricultural cooperatives, for example, was organized by the Dominican Republic. A video (made by the D.R.'s Vice President's office) featured some co-op members. One rural woman says, 'Our life was difficult before this project'. Another says: 'We learned about healthy eating. We learned how to sell our eggplants and our lettuce. ... The community can feed itself'. Her husband adds: 'People work for the well-being of the community. A woman in a fish culture project says, I see my fish so happy when I feed them. I feel as happy as they do'!

This session conveyed a further message: that the Dominican Republic is self-sufficient in food. A Member of Parliament, Luz Adelma, said that 'Most of the food crops in the Dominican Republic – rice and beans – are varieties locally obtained. We do not import any seeds.' She made an oblique reference to "conflict" generated by the seed law. She suggested that change might occur -- that, 'The market may open internationally', that 'many interests' were involved.

The significance of these comments became clear to me in another session, where a woman (Mercia Andrews) working in ten southern African countries talked about the harmful effects of multi-national corporations on food security and environment. Large corporations promote mono-cropping and use more fertilizer and pesticide than smaller farmers do.

African farmers – many of them women – traditionally produce, trade and bank their own seeds, Ms. Andrews explained. With the arrival of multinationals, however, 'Control over distribution, production, and rehabilitation of seeds has been increasingly taken over' by the Monsanto Corporation.

'Farmer-managed seed systems are no longer legal in Malawi', she said. 'We have to make sure that our seeds are registered'. Her organization, the Rural Women's Assembly, is resisting this move and searching for positive alternatives. 'We continue to grow our own seeds', she said, though they are under attack by state-supported multinationals.

An East and Southeast Asian women's organization organized a session describing their programs in five different countries – Japan, Taiwan, Sarawak, Philippines, and New Zealand. The theme of cooperatives came up again in relation to Japan, where panelists said that many young people are returning to the land, leaving rural areas to get training in agriculture, and forming cooperatives to market their goods. A program in Taiwan trains women in home maintenance skills, using tools and methods – tasks otherwise done by men.

Indigenous activism got a boost from the U.N.'s 2010 Declaration on the Rights of Indigenous People. This session was sponsored by an organization called The Codie Institute, which provides mentorship and training opportunities to American Indian women in the U.S. and Canada. One of the women recited her own poem, "Still I Fly," based on "Still I Rise," a poem by the African American writer Maya Angelou which stated:

> *You may shoot me with your words,*
> *You may cut me with your eyes.*
> *You may kill me with your hatefulness,*
> *But still, like air, I'll rise.*

An interesting aspect of this session was its emphasis on solving emotional problems of socially marginalized people.  One woman in the group, Patricia Thompson, introduced herself by saying, "I am a survivor. I am resilient." Two generations ago, she explained, 'We lost our language', she reminded us, because of Indian children being forced to go to boarding schools. Her father's mother was brutally murdered. She is now a grandmother of nine. "They are my legacy, the seeds I want to plant," she exclaimed. 'What can I do to make sure that my grandchildren do not feel fear or low esteem?' she asked. 'I want them to walk into a room with confidence. I want them to have the skills they need to nurture themselves'. Her "call to action" was: "Support each other... Help someone.... Provide presence when someone feels alone.... Provide safety when one feels helpless."

Her co-panelist, Joline, made a statement echoed by other indigenous speakers: "My indigenous values and knowledge can do much for the world." She added later, 'We need to recognize the contributions of indigenous people, not just shed tears over their problems'. This point came up in connection with promoting respect for the environment and finding ways to combat climate change.

Another indigenous group represented at this conference was the Sami, reindeer herders of northern Scandinavia. (I don't usually think of Europe as having "indigenous people," though there is some possibility that my own Swedish grandfather had a Sami connection.) The Sami women at this conference were highly organized and confident. But they talked about some of the same issues that the American Indian women did, especially feelings of shame about their low social status and being discouraged from speaking their native language.

One presentation stressed the need to collect the stories of Sami families in World War II while the elders are still alive. The interviewer, Liv Somby, mentioned that the woman she was interviewing assumed that Ms. Somby was making all her children's clothing, including their leather boots!

Danger is a regular theme at these meetings. Women from conflict areas come seeking support from an international community. Two years ago I was one of only two or three Americans in a session organized by women of South Sudan. They were visibly grateful that I was there, listening to them. Afterwards they surrounded me and thanked me for coming. I felt awkward and sad, that there weren't more influential people there to help them solve their terrible problems of war, displacement, and hunger.

There were passionate statements by two refugees, Ketty Nivyabandi from Burundi and Wai Wai Nu from the Myanmar Rohingyas. Both women now live in Canada. Ms. Nivyabandi fled Burundi in 2015 after a failed coup attempt. The head of state was illegally planning to run for a third term, and she organized the first women-only protest. One of her friends was gang-raped to death. She got out somehow, but others who remain there are being 'thoroughly terrorized', she said. She pleaded with her audience that, 'Only a *global* movement for human rights can counter this kind of injustice. We need to make the human rights struggle something "normal," something ordinary people can join, to bring about needed change'. She asked for help from the international community, saying, 'One country's people cannot do it on their own'.

Wai Wai Nu's community, the Rohingya, is now experiencing genocide in Myanmar (Burma). Those speaking up about it have been harassed and threatened. Social media are being used to humiliate activists and human rights defenders, she said. They are "criminalized" in many ways. (Joan Carling, the Special Rapporteur in the Philippines, has been labelled as a "terrorist" by the Philippine authorities.) Wai Wai Nu begged us to understand the terrible risks faced by people who stand up for rights, ordinary people. "We need to come up with a strong strategy and action plan to protect women on the ground," she said.

One reason why some women come to these meetings in New York is to meet personally with their own government embassy people. Apparently, they find they have better access to government officials in New York than they do back home. Several speakers urged participants to meet their own governmental representatives while they were in New York, to pressure them to follow through on commitments such as the Convention on the Elimination of All Forms of Discrimination Against Women (CEDAW).

Speaking of governments and their systems, the international NGO, ActionAid, is trying to mobilize support in several countries for counting unpaid care work as part of a country's "economy." ActionAid has calculated of the economic value of work such as child care, water collection, elder care, and so on. But these kinds of activities are not considered to have "economic value." (A speaker in another session, Dr. Maria Luisa Mendonca, pointed out that small-scale agriculture also does not usually count toward a country's GDP.) Not recognizing the economic value of care work feeds the illusion that women are less "valuable" than men.

One issue that has come up for special scrutiny in the last 20 years or so is "female genital mutilation," the custom (practiced widely in parts of Africa and the Middle East) of cutting out some of a girl's genitalia. The cutting is done by other women, usually around the time of puberty or somewhat before. The practice was once called "female circumcision," now it's FGM. In the places that follow this custom, being accepted as a proper woman (and getting married) depends on having it done. Apparently it is common for a girl to drop out of school, marry, and start her family after going through the ceremony. (I encountered this practice on a 1995 assignment for CARE in Sudan, but it was clearly not an issue to be handled by outsiders.)

This Maasai girl, Nice Leng'ete, has been working in her East African pastoralist community to create alternatives to FGM. She has many ideas about how to persuade her people that it is not only physically harmful for girls, but also that girls should stay in school rather than marrying when they are young adolescents. One of her local "education" strategies is to show school boys actual pictures of the operation being performed. (It's a secret, female-controlled ritual they would otherwise not see.) 'Boys, protect your sisters', she exclaims in one video.

Her approach is to create alternative ways for school girls to transition into womanhood without FGM. She showed a picture of a group of school girls being blessed by elders. They were doing this instead of being "circumcised." "Today we become women on the inside," they said.

This is an interesting example of what some anthropologists have called the "vernacularization" of the global human rights discourse. An internationally disputed practice is not just banned: it is replaced with a less "harmful" practice that serves a similar social purpose. UN Women is reaching out to private companies to promote gender equality in the workplace. Their platform of "Women's Empowerment Principles" was featured in one of the sessions. This is a somewhat unusual program, as the U.N. works more often with governments than with the private sector. (This is changing, but that's a different subject.)

In her introduction, the Chair of the Commission on the Status of Women, Geraldine Byrne Nason (delegate from Ireland), argued for "international labor standards" and "getting more women to the decision-making tables." (This initiative is the result  of collaboration between the U.N. Global Compact and U.N. Women.)

A representative of the U.S. Labor Department's Women's Bureau declared that, "A labor force model that isn't working for everyone isn't working at all." She argued that we need to do two things: change the model and change the dialogue. Assumptions of paid and unpaid "work" need to change.

Around 1500 companies have signed a CEO's pledge to uphold the UN's Women's Empowerment Principles. Microsoft and Citibank are among them. A few companies have "scored" themselves in terms of gender equity. The average score is 26 out of a possible 100.

Sexual harassment in the workplace was a major topic of discussion in this session: Padma Lakshmi, a well known Indian model, talked about this. She had been sexually abused as a child. "I teach my child," she said, "that her body is her own. I don't want to scare her. The tools I give her will help her succeed without fear."

Private companies had a chance to look good in that session, but a Brazilian activist, Dr. Maria Luisa Mendonça, talked about an ominous trend – the expansion of large corporations into the land market after the 2008 financial collapse, especially in Brazil. Large tracts of land are used for mono-crop agriculture, mining, or other profitable enterprises. Private militias defend these activities. Local populations are driven out and migrate to urban slums. Though Dr. Mendonca talked mainly about Brazil, the speaker I heard talking about seed banking in southern Africa (Mercia Andrews) was describing a similar process. She said that southern Africa has a "resource curse." The region attracts extractive industries, she said. And these threaten biodiversity and eradicate small-scale farming.

This conference included more discussion of United States problems than others I have attended – especially racial discrimination in the rural U.S. (the conference theme was Rural Women). At the inaugural session, an African American farmer, Ruth Faircloth, spoke about racist abuses continuing in force in her upstate New York community. Things that were "normal" 60 years ago, she said, are still happening today. If an African American person is in line at a store, she said, a White person can butt in front of them. The "N" word is still in use. Her organization (Rural Migrant Ministry) works on housing and helps women to vote (an empowering act). Rural women are more isolated than others, she said, and they suffer more domestic violence. 'Their men come home after long, humiliating work days and beat their wives, to make themselves feel like real men', she said. Like some of the refugees and others I heard, she was happy to have an opportunity to speak to this international audience and seemed hopeful about getting some kind of support from the assembled group.

Dr. Inga Winkler – a specialist on water and sanitation – described her research in a rural Alabama community whose population is around 70% African American. She argued that forcing rural homeowners to pay for their own septic systems effectively "criminalized" rural people for their lack of public sewerage services.

American writers and leaders have inspired women in far-away places. Maya Angelou, Toni Morrison, and the New York political activist, Bella Abzug – all were mentioned more than once in the sessions I attended. Especially moving was the young American Indian woman I talked about earlier, who wrote her own poem based on Maya Angelou's "Still I Rise."

In San Francisco and Los Angeles CEDAW is now law. In California alone, there are 19 county and city Commissions for Women, including one in Pasadena. There is a National Association of Commissions for Women.

Implementing CEDAW and other such rights,agreements, demands much from the states that have ratified them – sometimes more than political will allows. Most of the state signatories to CEDAW have made changes, such as establishing Ministries of Women's Affairs and passing legislation to support women's voting and property rights or oppose violence against women. These are slow processes, however. There are economic, political, and cultural obstacles to acceptance of these rights mandates.

Indigenous people who are proud of their own traditions have been having their own conversation about this too. Some have decided (with encouragement from the U.N.) to get involved. There is a serious need for cultural fine-tuning, but the world is getting smaller. Almost everyone is now subject to the same global political and economic pressures. It may be high time to get real about some basic human rights. If their governments can't muster the political will to do it for them, perhaps women and their organizations can do it for themselves.

## Suzanne and Veena

# Chapter IV
# Fifty Fifty by 2030

*Dialogue is more effective than debate. We need "conversations."*
                                                    –Urvashi Gandhi

A session which we were very keen to attend was the 'Leaving No One Behind for Planet 50-50 by 2030' where the theme was that every rural woman and girl would be everywhere. The session was a vibrant inter sectional and inter-generational conversation on what it will take to leave no rural woman or girl behind in the quest for a 50-50 planet. UN Women's Executive Director Phumzile Mlambo-Ngcuka was in the chair and we three were very much interested. We had collected the passes and the invites but when we went there, the conference room was overflowing and we could not even enter.

UN Women's flagship event: UN Women partnered with an extensive group of civil society organisations to hold an innovative flagship event enabling and empowering women from across all rural areas and all parts of the globe to have a voice. More importantly it was titled 'Leaving No One Behind', the slogan for the implementation of the SDGs.

Over 400 participants sat at round tables to listen and contribute their experiences from across the diversity of women in rural locations who were feeling at this point well and truly left behind. The list regrettably is long: widows, LGBTI, Indigenous, disability, migrant/refugees and these are not in themselves homogenous groups.

A great deal was said about intersectionality – recognising that individuals cannot be categorised with simple language. Everyone faces a complexity of challenges, but most especially those who are the weakest, the most vulnerable across all societies.

Although we listened to the voices and personal stories of many speakers, we were asked around our tables to look for positive recommendations for action. We all know what the challenges are but what can actually be done to move people out of poverty, to provide access to education, to offer facilities to ensure a healthy community? What do we need to do to bridge the gap between rhetoric and reality?

Answers came from 30 tables, some overlapping, many offering different solutions. It was clear there is a lot of frustration and feelings of powerlessness, as well as anger. Never was it more clear that #The Time Is Now.

The women in the room (and a few men) were determined that change must come – they are fed up of waiting. Phumzile Mlambo-Ngcuka Executive Director of UN Women has been clear all week repeatedly saying 'The world has reached a tipping point'.

The final challenge of the day was more personal. What are we, as activists and individuals, going to do to make sure no one is left behind? We must continue to raise our voices, to make sure our organisations are strong and working toward achieving the 2030 Agenda but most of all, as individuals, we must ensure we change the world for at least one woman, one girl.

***UN Women Executive Director Phumzile Mlambo-Ngcuka had said on International Women's Day, 8 March 2017:***

"Across the world, too many women and girls spend too many hours on household responsibilities—typically more than double the time spent by men and boys. Women look after younger siblings, older family members, deal with illness in the family and manage the house. In many cases this unequal division of labour is at the expense of women's and girls' learning, of paid work, sports, or engagement in civic or community leadership. This shapes the norms of relative disadvantage and advantage, of where women and men are positioned in the economy, of what they are skilled to do and where they will work.

This is the unchanging world of unrewarded work, a globally familiar scene of withered futures, where girls and their mothers sustain the family with free labour, with lives whose trajectories are very different from the men of the household.

We want to construct a different world of work for women. As they grow up, girls must be exposed to a broad range of careers, and encouraged to make choices that lead beyond the traditional service and care options to jobs in industry, art, public service, modern agriculture and science.

We have to start the change at home and in the earliest days of school, so that there are no places in a child's environment where they learn that girls must be less, have less, and dream smaller than boys.

This will take adjustments in parenting, curricula, educational settings, and channels for everyday stereotypes like TV, advertising and entertainment; it will take determined steps to protect young girls from harmful cultural practices like early marriage, and from all forms of violence.

Women and girls must be ready to be part of the digital revolution. Currently only 18 per cent of undergraduate computer science degrees are held by women. We must see a significant shift in girls all over the world taking STEM (*Science, Technology, Engineering, and Mathematics*) subjects, if women are to compete successfully for high-paying 'new collar' jobs. Currently just 25 per cent of the digital industries' workforce is women.

Achieving equality in the workplace will require an expansion of decent work and employment opportunities, involving governments' targeted efforts to promote women's participation in economic life, the support of important collectives like trade unions, and the voices of women themselves in framing solutions to overcome current barriers to women's participation, as examined by the UN Secretary-General's High-level Panel on Women's Economic Empowerment. The stakes are high: advancing women's equality could boost global GDP by US$12 trillion by 2025.

It also requires a determined focus on removing the discrimination women face on multiple and intersecting fronts over and above their gender: sexual orientation, disability, older age, and race. Wage inequality follows these: the average gender wage gap is 23 per cent but this rises to 40 per cent for African American women in the United States. In the European Union, elderly women are 37 per cent more likely to live in poverty than elderly men.

In roles where women are already over-represented but poorly paid, and with little or no social protection, we must make those industries work better for women. For example, a robust care economy that responds to the needs of women and gainfully employs them; equal terms and conditions for women's paid work and unpaid work; and support for women entrepreneurs, including their access to finance and markets. Women in the informal sector also need their contributions to be acknowledged and protected. This calls for enabling macroeconomic policies that contribute to inclusive growth and significantly accelerate progress for the 770 million people living in extreme poverty.

Addressing the injustices will take resolve and flexibility from both public and private sector employers. Incentives will be needed to recruit and retain female workers; like expanded maternity benefits for women that also support their re-entry into work, adoption of the Women's Empowerment Principles , and direct representation at decision-making levels. Accompanying this, important changes in the provision of benefits for new fathers are needed, along with the cultural shifts that make uptake of paternity and parental leave a viable choice, and thus a real shared benefit for the family.

In this complexity there are simple, big changes that must be made: for men to parent, for women to participate and for girls to be free to grow up equal to boys. Adjustments must happen on all sides if we are to increase the number of people able to engage in decent work, to keep this pool inclusive, and to realize the benefits that will come to all from the equal world envisaged in our Agenda 2030 for Sustainable Development."

For too long a period, majority of women round the world have been subjected to atrocities, not given a chance to voice their feelings, or realize their dreams or hope for equal treatment. In a male dominated patriarchal society, women have been left lagging behind, following in the footsteps of their male members and not allowed to reach their full potential.

Of course there are a small minority who have stood up and fought for their rights. But it is a small minority and not the majority. And these women have been either treated as heroines or squashed down and trampled upon.

These may be strong words, but listening to women round the world during the recent CSW62 organised by the United Nations from March 12 to March 23, 2018, I have come to the conclusion that all women of the world face similar problems. Urban or rural, rich or poor, white, black, brown or yellow, all women have suffered and are suffering for no fault of theirs, except being of the female gender.

More than 4,300 representatives from over 600 civil society organizations, and 170 Member States attended this year's Commission. These figures represent a steady increase from previous year's participation showing a growing strength and unity of women's voices around the world, and showcase the potential for civil society to leverage the agreed conclusions in their mission to hold governments accountable. Women came, spoke, listened and went back to their respective countries full of ideas and plans to make the world a better place from women, urban and rural.

The Commission is one of the largest annual gatherings of global leaders, NGOs, private sector actors, United Nations partners and activists from around the world focusing on the status of rights and empowerment of all women and girls, everywhere.

Today when education and enlightenment has made many a man realize that half the population of the world is filled by the fair sex, they have started taking some notice. Women now demand a fifty percent in all spheres and have set the goal of 2030 to achieve this through requests, demands, fights, complaints and so on.

Educate, empower, enable women, says the Soroptimist International (SI) group which is a global network of 75,000 women who work together at local, national and international levels, transforming the lives of women and girls. SI has been in existence from 1921 and is active in 122 countries with 19 UN representatives at 6 UN centres. It focuses on quality education, gender equality and clean water and sanitation.

SI says that women are powerful force for change and dedicates itself to promoting, encouraging and positioning women to have an equal voice in creating strong, sustainable and peaceful communities the world over. SI is a global voice for women and in Kenya, it works with the Mwihoko Women in supporting women to move into commercial farming, investing in water tanks, new technologies and hands-on skills training. In Nepal, twenty projects wherein girls are given scholarships to attend school, computer literacy programs, hygiene education, trauma counseling, reintegration programs for survivors of trafficking.

The See Solar, Cook Solar (2013-2015) project has benefitted 6000 women and girls across three continents through seven projects.

Similar projects round the world are going on at full steam to make the Fifty-fifty by 2030 dream become a reality.

During the 'Leaving No One Behind for Planet 50-50 by 2030' the UN women and partners held a vibrant intersectional and intergenerational conversation on what it will take to leave no rural woman or girl behind in the quest for a 50-50 planet.

During the concluding session, UN Women's Executive Director Phumzile Mlambo-Ngcuka declared:

"I want to thank you for the resolutions that were adopted this evening and for the agreed conclusions, which go far in enabling us to address the very special situation that is faced by women and girls in rural areas.

These agreed conclusions focus on addressing the poverty of women and girls in rural areas; the important issue of access, ownership and control of land and other productive resources; opportunities and challenges in agriculture, including their food security and nutrition; and they also recognize that the lives of women in rural areas are not only confined to food production and agriculture. They address the impact of climate change, and the need for infrastructure such as for ICT, energy, transport, drinking water and sanitation.

They importantly address education, from childhood education to tertiary education, including vocational training and lifelong learning. This is both a right and a tool to enhance their varied roles in the economy and in public life.

They address unpaid care and domestic work and ensure that we prioritize the recognition of the need to reduce and redistribute women's work and to recognize unpaid work in our economies.

They address social protection policies, and access to affordable and quality social services, including child-care services, maternity, paternity or parental leave.

They recognize multiple and intersecting forms of discrimination, and the protection, rights and needs of indigenous women, women with disabilities, women of African descent, older women, as well as young women and girls in rural areas.

They require us to ensure that we use the resources and partnerships that we have to respond to the needs identified.

They also raise the importance of laws that end all forms of discrimination against women and girls in rural areas and the norms that underlie them.

They capture the fact that this is a tipping point. In the last few weeks we have discussed the notion that it is time to end all forms of gender inequality.

The youth here, in particular, captured the urgency of the moment. In their own deliberations they have asked us to highlight the fact that they believe in, and are committed to, taking an active role in their destiny. They highlighted the importance of being present and participating fully, as the women in rural areas also highlighted, where there are issues that impact on their lives and that are being deliberated.

They have asked that we continue to have them in our delegations, thanked those delegations that did involve young women in the future they are discussing and urged those who did not, to do so. They told me that I will not be around to enjoy that future, so I should make sure that they are there to represent themselves.

They made very strong points about the need for access to education, such as stigma-free comprehensive sexuality education, access to affordable digital connections and technology, and safe online interactions.

Young women committed themselves to protect the environment, to climate justice and to full participation in the political lives of their countries. They emphasized the importance of working in an intergenerational context so that they can learn from those who have been around for much longer, and so that they can contribute to advising us and giving us direction for the future.

In conclusion, as we work to ensure that we leave no one behind, the theme that we have discussed this year is probably one of the most important because women who live in rural areas are at higher risk of being left behind. Our ability to address the needs of women and girls who are living in rural areas is the biggest contribution we can make to ensure the Sustainable Development Goals are achieved in the best possible way for the majority of humanity."

The closing remarks by other officials were:

"Women and girls who live in rural areas are not at the danger of being left behind, they ARE being left behind," said Lopa Banerjee, Director of the Civil Society Division at UN Women, opening the Youth Dialogue hosted on 17 March, at the 62nd Commission on the Status of Women. The Dialogue, focusing on the theme, "Leave No One Behind", witnessed spirited discussions revolving around the challenges and opportunities in achieving gender equality and the empowerment of young women and girls living in rural communities, and was led by UN Women in collaboration with the UN Youth Envoy and nine civil society organizations.

"As young people, what all of us need to understand is that using our voice doesn't cost anything," said Jaha Dukureh, anti-FGM activist from The Gambia, and now UN Women's Regional Goodwill Ambassador for Africa, emphasizing on the importance of solidarity among the youth.

The UN's largest annual gathering on gender equality and women's rights concluded in New York with the strong commitment by UN Member States to achieving gender equality and the empowerment of rural women and girls. Coming on the heels of unprecedented global activism and public outcry to end gender injustice and discrimination worldwide, the 62nd session of the UN Commission on the Status of Women (CSW) reached a robust agreement highlighting the urgency of empowering and supporting those who need it most and have, for too long, been left behind.

The outcome of the two-week meeting, known as the Agreed Conclusions adopted by Member States, puts forth concrete measures to lift rural women and girls out of poverty and to ensure their rights, well-being and resilience. These include ensuring their adequate living standards with equal access to land and productive assets, ending poverty, enhancing their food security and nutrition, decent work, infrastructure and technology, education and health, including their sexual and reproductive health and reproductive rights, and ending all forms of violence and harmful practices. Member States recognize in the conclusions rural women's important role in addressing hunger and food insecurity. This strong outcome provides a roadmap on next steps that governments, civil society and women's groups can undertake to support the realization of rural women's rights and address their needs.

The Executive Director of UN Women, which serves as the CSW Secretariat, Phumzile Mlambo-Ngcuka, said: "The

Commission's agreement on measures to bring substantive equality to women and girls in rural areas is a vital step forward. In the Commission's two weeks of dialogue we have heard clearly from the women and girls themselves what they want: from the rights to own property, to the need for quality infrastructure, to the rights to make decisions about their own bodies and lives. Effective action to bring the changes they need will take the continued engagement of all partners, from governments to civil society. Rural women themselves must be able to speak up and be heard in all consultations, and youth delegations must be included at all levels. These agreements are made in the meeting rooms of New York but must take effect in the lives of women and girls we are here to serve."

In its final agreement, the Commission emphasized that rural women and girls are essential to sustainable development, and their rights and empowerment needs to be prioritized. A broad range of concrete next steps and recommendations were outlined in the Agreed Conclusions.

They include:

- Adoption of reforms to eliminate discriminatory laws and norms for women to have equal access to economic and productive resources, including land and natural resources, property and inheritance rights.

- Step up progress towards strong educational environments at all levels including closing gender gaps in secondary and tertiary education in rural areas.

- Provision of quality social services, and care services, to reduce the disproportionate share of unpaid care and domestic work of rural women and girls.

- Ensuring rural women have access to decent jobs with equal pay for work of equal value, and that they participate equally in all decisions, from households to community forums.

- Increasing essential rural infrastructure and technology, which typically reach rural women last, by providing access to, for instance, safe drinking water, a clean stove, sanitation facilities and connectivity.

- Stepping up investments to ensure their food security and nutrition and the increased financial inclusion and access to financial services of women farmers.

- Provision of universal health coverage, and realizing the need for women and girls in rural areas to manage and exercise their sexual and reproductive health.

- Accelerate action to end all forms of violence against women, including harmful practices such as child marriage and female genital mutilation.

"The world will never realize 100 per cent of its goals if 50 per cent of its people cannot realize their full potential. When we unleash the power of women, we can secure the future for all." *Ban Ki-moon, UN Secretary-General 2015.*

**Phumzile Mlambo-Ngcuka,**

**CSW session in progress**

# Chapter V
# Impressions of Delegates

*There is a culture of silence, a reluctance to discuss internal conflicts with outsiders. Victims face "shame and blame"*
— Hanne Bjurstrom

- **Dr Padmini Murthy**
  Professor/Global Health Director NYMC SHSP
  MWIA Addl NGO Rep to United Nations
  Executive Committee NGOCSW NY to United Nations
  Governing Councilor International Health Section APHA
  Sr Fellow Public Private Alliance Foundation

Dr Murthy is Millennium Milestone Maker Awardee and has been awarded the prestigious Blackwell Medal by the American Medical Women's Association (AMWA) which is conferred as recognition of service provided by women physicians and she is the first Indian born American to get this honor since its inception since 1949.

In March 1999 I first had the opportunity of attending the CSW in New York City and this has been the beginning of one of the best experiences I have had. The 2 week long program which is orchestrated by the United Nations every year in March is the venue for one of largest gathering of women from all corners of the world to meet, network, discuss and address issues of importance to them. Before the creation of UN Women in 2010 the Division of Advancement of Women – DAW and United

Nations Development Fund for Women (UNIFEM) were the focal points for the CSW every year.

I have had the honor of being on the NGOCSW committee in New York for the past 6 years and have been actively involved in working on organizing the parallel events to commemorate the CSW every year. The NGO CSW committee in New York works closely with the UN Women to organize the various parallel events, Consultation day, Reception, Celebration March and the Artisan Fair every year. I have served as Co-chair of the Reception committee, Woman of Distinction Award committee, and Artisan Fair committee for the past 6 years. I have interacted with various NGO colleagues from various countries, met women who are trailblazers and made a difference in their communities and worldwide. One such woman who made a lasting impression on me is Noble laureate Leymah Gowbee and I had the privilege of meeting and working with to send Safe Motherhood Kits to Liberia. In addition, working on the various committees has taught me to believe in team work and respect cultural diversity and have helped to develop my people skills when interacting with others in all walks of life whether it is professional or personal.

I try to attend as many parallel events I can every year in addition to those I organize with my NGO co representative to the United Nations on behalf of my NGO Medical Women's International Association. For the past 12 years. I have also had the privilege of being invited to speak on behalf of NGOs at a high level event the United Nations during the CSW a few years ago.

The CSW has been a great platform for me to work with colleagues from the UN and Ambassadors of various countries to the United Nations. In 2016 February on behalf of the NGO CSW committee in NY I had the privilege of chairing the Women Ambassadors Luncheon at the Hungarian Mission under the patronage of HE Ambassador Bogyay of Hungary to the United Nations. This celebratory event in which the women ambassadors to the United Nations were honored was a fore runner to the upcoming CSW.

I have also over the past 15 years encouraged my graduate and medical students to attend the CSW parallel events as it a great educational opportunity. I am proud that my daughter and her friends as youth representatives were active organizers in the youth CSW which was held in 2017 under the auspices of UN Women. It is indeed gratifying to see the number of youth participants increasing at the CSW playing varied roles as attendees, speakers, organizers and future change makers and advocates.

In conclusion I would encourage my fellow global citizens to attend the CSW if the opportunity arises at least once as it is a unique and life changing experience.

- **Fenna Bacchus,**
  CEO, Viva Green Bio Technologies, Inc. (NGO, International Consultant):

During the UNCSW 62, I established contact with Mariam Mohamed Adam from Elruhama Organization for Development and Humanitarian Aid, accompanied by Sudan's Prime Minister's wife. This paves the way for Viva Green Bio Technologies to work in Sudan, Darfur where we have over 200,000 women and children refugees. These refugees are involved in income generating activities. CSW has given me the global platform to meet such unique women-owned NGO's to feature our Agricultural Technologies that will benefit rural farmers.

Honorable Zoe Bakoko Bakoru, former Ugandan Minister of Gender Labour and Social Development introduced Viva Green Bio Technologies to the African Union Member States. CSW has given a global platform to establish initial contact with NGOs that paves the way to feature Agricultural Technologies. This will greatly benefit rural farmers in Africa. It's instructive that scientists are also from the African continent

I met Nozala Trust from South Africa for partnering with their start up program in Mpumalanga Province, Vukuzakhe Gardens. I also established contact with The National Council of Women of Indonesia, KOWANI, Ibu Heni Handayani Yakob and Ibu Lr Sharmila for partnership. Viva Green Bio Technologies is looking forward to enter Indonesia.

I met Khoboso Harguru Adichareh, the founder of Kargi Pastoralist Link, a Foundation based in the UK for partnering with their organization. Viva Green Bio Technologies is happy to on the ground in Kenya and plans to enter Tanzania. We plan to start work with the pastoralists communities in Kenya and Tanzania

I had the privilege of meeting one of the most powerful women activists in the world, Otilia Lux de Cotí. Like me, she definitely was a power house that holds governments accountable. Our goal is to involve co-ops of community-based grassroots organizations around the world to establish Small-Scale Bio factories for production of Bio products for small holder agriculture production. We shall achieve this by innovating low input technologies that use local materials and provide some sort of value addition to ensure sustainability and food security. This will provide a sustainable livelihood for the poor while drastically reducing greenhouse gas emissions that pose a looming threat to climate change for the most vulnerable populations especially those in slums and low lying areas in the world –

- **Dr. Suzanne Hanchett,**
  Planning Alternatives for Change, LLC
  Freelance social development consultant since 1991. Her
  specialties are gender equity, poverty related issues, and
  WASH (water, sanitation, hygiene). PAC Partner:

While attending 23 of the hundreds of Side- and Parallel-Events held during the two week meetings of the Commission on the Status of Women, I took notes that were as detailed as possible. These notes are simply a record of what was said. Writing down these statements does not mean that I agree with everything that people said. I wanted the notes to reflect proceedings as clearly as possible, so that readers could know how it felt to be in those rooms. My own wish to understand what approaches do or do not work for rural women's social development influenced my selection of panels. I am very interested in socially marginalized people and their struggles to improve their lot, so I emphasized the sessions on indigenous people too. I did not follow other threads: child marriage or domestic violence, for example. Of course, just saying that an organization or approach is working does not mean that it is working. The stakes are high at this type of meeting. NGOs and others need to look as good as they can. Their reputations are affected by these presentations.

And in the fundraising business, reputation is very important. Certain common themes were repeated in many of these sessions. Rural women's need to learn about their legal rights was one. The importance of girls' and women's education/ training and skill development was stressed over and over again. Speakers talked about organizational strategies. Specific governments' actions/inaction relative to the Sustainable Development Goals (SDG) was another one. Ominous trends, such as state-backed takeovers of land by investors, were mentioned by several speakers.

These trends are related to the spread of agribusiness and monocropping, which challenge (even may criminalize) local people's use of their own seeds, mining interests and other large-scale businesses with environmental impacts. Small-holder women and their leaders were trying to find a way to express their alarm about these trends at this meeting. Meanwhile, the UN is trying to bring in the "private sector," to make it part of the solution to women's rights and other international labor problems. Women in exile, whose lives were in danger, expressed hope that "the international community" would come to the aid of human rights defenders.

Some of the people who spoke at this meeting have had their lives threatened by agents of their own governments. My notes cover some of the questions asked by audience members. Not all of these questions were answered. At the March 16 meetings in support of agricultural cooperatives, for example, one person pointed out that in her African country cooperatives are not working properly. This question deserves attention. Just saying that they work does not mean they work exactly the same, or exactly as well, under all conditions. Another unanswered question was asked at the March 23 panel hosted by the International Women's Anthropology Conference. It concerned the long-term viability of NGOs. Many NGO leaders, the questioner said, are themselves economically insecure. She sought ideas about how grassroots groups, or coalitions, can achieve the financial stability they need to keep up their work. There was not enough time in the panel to give this question the time it deserves.

- **Anuradha Pradeep**
  India, Ministry of Women and child development

**'The integral education of rural girls and women':** This event was a very well presented event, the main speakers were quite experienced in their field of work, the hall was over crowded well before the event could start, I thought the presence of the

Archbishop Bernardito Auza made the difference, the event was in partnership with Catholic Women's Forum and so there were many institutions and their students present for the event.

The first speaker was Mary Hasson from Fuller Sense of Empowerment of Women through Education and an Author, other than this she had many accomplishments to her credit and she herself was mother of 7 children. She said that if world as a whole is taken then percentage wise it can be definitely said that there is parity in education in all levels, but the important thing is that it is unevenly distributed like in many regions of the world there is a huge disparity and so focus is to be given to these countries etc.  She was proposing a "Person Centric Education' in other words to recognize the dignity of the women through education. Not all the women in the world need to complete their schooling while going to school is important they need to empower themselves in such a way that they are respected in what they choose to do.

Sakeena Yacoobi, is an ordinary Afghan woman who has fought for education in Afghanistan. She narrated the manner in which she was able to achieve a breakthrough in setting up schools in Afghanistan. She said that even in the existing schools then there were no female teachers at all. After her 25 years of struggle she was proud to announce that in one year they were able to bring 15,000 children to schools, though there were no statistics declared, there was a lot of work that has happened and education in Afghanistan has become a reality.

Amritpal Sandhu from a Fund for education in Emergencies which under the campaign "Education cannot wait" spoke about how the fund works in providing education in emergencies. Afghanistan was the example for them as well.  A film made in association with UNICEF was shown where women expressed their wish to learn and how role of father is important in educating a girl child.

Timorthy Raricle- a father himself spoke from the point of view of a father and the need for educating a girl child. There is a need for Men and Fathers to play a great role in empowerment of Women and girls whether rural or otherwise. The CSW should make more efforts to rope in more and more men to be a part of the discussions; this will see more men coming for the events and will give a new dimension to the mission of women which is going on.

- **Dr Shivani Khetan,
  Tarot Card reader**

My experience at the 62 Commission On the Status of Women with my fantastic colleagues Dr Veena Adige and Dr Jayshree Borad:

Over the last two weeks, and during my first delegation as a NGO representative of Zoroastrian college to the Commission on the status of women (CSW) at the United Nations, I participated in official events participated by country missions and UN agencies on diverse matters, including ending child marriage, closing gender gap in agriculture, violence against women, encouraging women for greater purpose, health, environmental degradation, gender equality programs and much much more. The best part about my time at the CSW was without a doubt the fascinating people I met. Without a question, my personal network has been enriched and blessed with amazing friends doing great work in their fields. The energy, excitement and exchange of ideas and appropriate steps to take for the issues to transform our passions into better world for all of us. Ringing the peace bell together, let's do everything in our powers to get there. Thank you Dr Meher Master-Moos for inspiring us and guiding us to work in the commission in other phases of our work lives. With your support, encouragement and guidance it has a positive impact on our lives and has provided us with unique experience of national exchange and good practice for bringing the voice of women movement to the women of the United Nations. It was an amazing experience to meet Queen Mother Dr Delois Blakely.

- ### Dr Jayshree Borad
  ### Geobiological consultant, Vedic Vaastu

CSW-62 has been the most profound experiences of my life. Meeting women from all walks of life, conversing with them made me realize that it is very important to work for the most primary right of women that is equality.

Planet 50-50 is the aim of UN but to achieve this we all will have to work hard in hand. I particularly appreciate the phrase "women from Rural" than using the term Rural women which sounds harsh and mean. There was such an awesome energy all around the event. The UN, NGOs and all Organisations had really worked hard to make this event such a grand success. I am grateful to UN for giving us this platform where we could meet successful women from all genre of life. There was great amount of learning and got a lot of clarity about the life of girl child and women around the world.

If a woman of the family is educated the next generation and the coming generations can benefit in great way. Only then can we make this planet a better place to live.

A special thanks to madam Dr. Meher, Dr.Veena, Dr. Shivani, Mrs Renu Reddy & Mrs Chitra Jain for making my CSW-62 and New York trip such an amazing one.

Three cheers for women empowerment!!!..

- **Dr Veena Adige:**
  **Journalist and Educator**

The Kaleidoscope of the thousands of women who attended the CSW62 revealed that women the world over have similar problems, solutions and thinking. The energy, the excitement and exchange of ideas can be transformed into a better world for all. Though women who live in rural areas are at a higher risk of being left behind, the 50-50 in 2030 can become a reality. I saw that there was no discrimination among the delegates, there were instant friendships made and there was laughter in the cafes but pin drop silence during the sessions. Temple of Understanding certainly paved the way to better understanding of people and situations. I enjoyed the whole program.

- **Rayner Rees**

I met so many interesting people from around the world and it made me realise just how many NGOs (non-government organisation) are working to improve the status of women and girls. By the end of the week, I had begun to enjoy every minute and now that I am home, I can honestly say that it was a wonderful experience and I can confirm that our Soroptimist organisation is a world leader in supporting women and girls across the globe.

Child marriage affects all aspects of life with rural girls who more likely to become child brides. There is a need to address gender equality and allow girls to make their own decisions although according to UNICEF there are decreasing numbers in child marriages. Problems such as prolonged labour can lead to fistulas, prolapse and hysterectomies and early death – all of which result in social stigma. In many countries there is a patriarchal society where marriage is glorified with beautiful clothes and jewelry and there is lack of access to contraceptives.

There can be little doubt that early marriage affects a girl's life path. Education is one way of combatting this by changing gender norms to this traditional problem and working with families and communities sharing information on contraception and dangers of early marriage. A change in attitude of traditional leaders, working with religious groups, including sex education in school curriculums, teaching boys to respect girls and government understanding of their role will all help to combat this problem.

- **Dr Bhavna Joshipura**
  President, AIWC, First Lady Mayor of Rajkot,
  Social worker, Rural women's reformer

It was really a very delightful experience to participate in CSW-62 at NYC – USA. I found during my visit that the women wanted to find their "soul and their self-respect" in a social environment created by man. I was happy to share my views on rural women empowerment, especially about converting the challenges into the opportunities - It was CFUW - where I was one of the speakers.

I was a speaker for IAW and was happy to speak on the rural women empowerment aspect. I felt that the organisers were very much eager to understand the ground level situation prevailing in my country.

I strongly feel that Rural India is the REAL India. My journey of acquainting myself with rural women began in 1983. But the sensitivity for it had started developing in 1965 when as a little girl of a small town of Surendranagar in Surendranagar district of Gujarat I used to fetch water from the river, and when the water was scarce, we used to make niches in the sandy river bed to get water.

When I started working among the rural women, I first started to mingle with them and talk to them. I realized that some of them were not even aware of their problems. Until 2002, my efforts were not much organized but three decades of work in that area gave me a specific insight to carry out the work.

During the course of travelling across the rural and mofussil areas for meeting with women workers, cooperatives and workers of specific work areas, I used to stop along the roadside whenever I saw women at work and entered into dialogue with them about their work, family situation and their day to day problems they had to face in their respective working areas. The women's responses were quite encouraging and they were cordial with visitors like me, usually they had a mother-in-law to help look after the children while at work, at the same time they had taught themselves special skills like sewing, embroidery, bid work, traditional art and pearl work and other skill or semi-skill works.

It is my firm belief that there are opportunities and avenues for Indian rural women such as;

- The way the women of rural areas are facing the challenges and providing essential service and support to the entire family substantiates that their innate strength is boundless and that is the major opportunity.

- The rural women possess traditional abilities, skills and talents. For instance, in Kutchh, a bordering district of western India, from an adolescent girl to an adult woman, all have inherited the art of world famous embroidery and knitting and this is one of the reasons - because of these ladies, Kutchh has found its place on the global canvas.

- In the Saurashtra region of Gujarat, most of the women, whether literate or illiterate know a sort of thread work called 'jardosi work', a type of knitting and embroidery called 'Khatli work', traditional embroidery, bead work, job work of silver jewellery, diamond work. Especially, in the areas around Jamnagar, Vadhwan and Jetpur, the women are well versed in the traditional work of 'bandhni' – a sort of art of tie and die; and in the interior parts of Saurashtra region, the women know the art of weaving saris called 'patola'. This work of art is practiced by women only. They get up around four in the morning to carry out this work. 'Bandhani' and 'Patola' saris are known all over the world.

- Apart from physical strength, these rural women also own qualities like assiduousness and conviction.

- The rural area contains ceaseless striving and toiling strength of women. If this ceaseless strength is honed with skill enhancement and equipped with vocational expertise, one can obtain quite encouraging results. Rural economy is based on agriculture. And animal husbandry is its major fraction. Under the current situation, the contribution of women is quite commendable.

After attending the CSW - 62; I have accelerated and expanded my area of working in Saurastra Region. We have been organizing medical camps. A network of Primary Health Centers already exists. We facilitated them to go and avail facilities available there. Simultaneously we also started conducting meetings for awareness for immunization and also provided free medicines and periodical follow-up programmes. During all such activities, we started educating them regarding various Government Schemes for health and hygiene. After some time, we realized that in order to achieve long lasting effects we should develop social leadership as well so that the entire Endeavour becomes sustainable and self-sufficient. Thus our efforts were overlapping, integrated and complimentary to one another.

To sum up, the secret of our success was we were able to sensitize them towards their issues and willingness to overcome them through persistent and planned efforts. Their involvement in the task was immense owing to their strong instinct of self existence. I salute their collective efforts. They prove the golden words of Swami Vivekananda –

***"Arise, Awake and stop not still the***
***goal is reached...." True.***

My entire UN CSW - 62 visit is very significant and I must mention that during this process, I have also learnt many things. It was not just giving on my part. It was giving and sharing process.

I am very much thankful towards AIWC central leadership I must express my sincere gratitude towards Ms. Manju Kak (India), Bobby Nasar, Cheryl Hyles, (CFUW), Joanna Mangannara (IAW).

My Participation as the Speaker - UN CSW - 62 NYC

1. Canadian Federation of University Women (Dt. 13-3-2018)

    Speakers :    1. Dr. Bhavna Joshipura

                      2. Terry Show

                      3. Paulette S

    Moderator : Charyl Hails

Dr. Bhavna Joshipura delivered the speech on the topic of "how to convert the challenges into the opportunities." It was very much interactive session.

Venue : The Armenian Convention Centre, Vartan hall

2. Parallel event of IAW

   Special Presence 1. Ms. Joana Magnara,

                  2. Ms.Chereyl,

                  3. Ms. Manju Kak,

                  4. Dr. Bhavna Joshipura,

   Moderator :      Ms. Yun Sun

3. Event of AIWC.

   Coordinator   :  Bobby Show

   Special Presence :  1. Yun Sun.

                  2. Mrs. Manju Kak

   Moderator     : Yun Sun

In this event I was very much delighted to be invited as the speaker and I have narrated some important aspects such as skill development, Grass root activities, self-help group etc.

- **Gail Neff**

It was an amazing experience to hear about the conditions of women in countries all over the world. To get an overview of this huge conference , I attended about five 90 min. panel discussions per day for 6 days!  I heard presentations from ambassadors, ministers, NGOs (Non-Governmental Organizations) and civil society (citizen activists) on a variety of topics including rural women in agriculture, land rights, inheritance rights, politics, education, access to internet and radio to reduce isolation and increase knowledge, child marriage, and violence to name just a few.  It produced a  whirlwind of information that I am still struggling to organize and communicate in a way that does justice to the issues.

In order to make successful change, advocates need to work together.  This is certainly facilitated by the annual Commission on the Status of Women.  It often involves partnering with groups in other countries.  This was evident in the variety of countries represented on most panels.  For example in the session Korea Against War,  the speakers were from Canada, Japan, and So. Korea.  They talked about their combined efforts to urge Foreign Ministers from 20 countries to keep peaceful negotiations as the only option for security on the Korean peninsula.  Other partnerships were between Afganistan and Finland, and Uganda and Australia.  Canada is also partnering with Kenya to help with setting up an Investment Fund using local savings to be used for local projects. In many of the presentations, there was a strong push to include women in decisions affecting their rights.

I was surprised to learn that in South Korea, there is 100% literacy, with 25% of the national budget earmarked for primary education.  One program feeds children at school to ensure they come, using food produced by local farmers which helps the local economy.

Another success story is in Rwanda, where in 1994, one million people were slaughtered in acts of genocide. The current President is a firm leader making good decisions and fast changes. All children are required to have 12 years of education. 90% are covered by health insurance and 90% with HIV are receiving medication. Life expectancy has increased from 48 to 67 and women are being encouraged to participate in government.

Other reports, however, were heartbreaking: Widows required to marry a brother-in-law or lose her children and be cast out of her home, children as young as 10 who were raped, were denied abortions because of religious customs, and of course, lack of penalties for violence against women. Small improvements in the lives of women and girls are being made in many countries but progress is discouragingly slow in most.

It is sobering for me to realize that in many countries, women are actually risking their lives when they advocate for gender equality and freedom from sexual assault and exploitation.

One lovely and unexpected meeting happened when another delegate and I were waiting for the next session to start. Three women came into the room to have some lunch, and when they saw us they offered to share their homemade Persian rice and stew. We accepted and discovered they were health workers in Iran who, among other activities, organized mobile clinics for rural areas. The one young woman who spoke excellent English was born in New York and had no trouble travelling between the US and Iran. Life in Iran seemed quite nice from their description.

The Woman of Distinction Award was given to an amazing, self-taught, Zulu grandmother named Sizani Ngubane, who founded The Rural Women Movement in South Africa. It now has 50,000 members who are learning how to advocate for women's rights. Her motto " persist, insist, and resist" has served her well. She noted that 80% of food production is done by women, but only 2% of the land is owned by women. So, in 1994, she decided to try to change the law. With other "unruly women", she took the government to court to allow women to own and inherit land. In 2010, she won the suit! She pointed out that there was still much to be done. Despite laws being on the books, local customs often impede their implementation.

Women in rural areas include migrant workers. They often don't know what their legal rights are and are afraid to report instances of abuse for fear of losing their jobs or being deported. Migrants in Florida are experiencing what is essentially modern day slavery. Laws are unable to stop abuses in the fields or for those in domestic care if not reported. I participated in a 4 hour protest march on the streets of New York in support of more protection for women agricultural and migrant workers so they can report abuses.

I attended as one of 20 delegates of the Canadian Federation of University Women (CFUW). Our combined comments will be used to lobby the Canadian Government.

# Chapter VI
## Benefits of Economic Empowerment of Women

*We have talked enough. It's time to act. Key actions are: land rights, gender responsive climate action ("Say nothing without consulting us"), and "Free, prior, and informed consent."*
— Agnes, a woman from Kenya

- When more women work, economies grow. An increase in female labour force participation—or a reduction in the gap between women's and men's labour force participation—results in faster economic growth.

- Evidence from a range of countries shows that increasing the share of household income controlled by women, either through their own earnings or cash transfers, changes spending in ways that benefit children.

- Increasing women and girls' education contributes to higher economic growth. Increased educational attainment accounts for about 50 per cent of the economic growth in OECD countries over the past 50 years, of which over half is due to girls having had access to higher levels of education and achieving greater equality in the number of years spent in education between men and women. But, for the majority of women, significant gains in education have not translated into better labour market outcomes.

- A study using data from 219 countries from 1970 to 2009 found that, for every one additional year of education for women of reproductive age, child mortality decreased by 9.5 per cent.

- Women tend to have less access to formal financial institutions and saving mechanisms. While 55 per cent of men report having an account at a formal financial institution, only 47 per cent of women do worldwide. This gap is largest among lower middle-income economies as well as in South Asia and the Middle East and North Africa.

## The world of work

- Women continue to participate in labour markets on an unequal basis with men. In 2013, the male employment-to-population ratio stood at 72.2 per cent, while the ratio for females was 47.1 per cent.

- Globally, women are paid less than men. Women in most countries earn on average only 60 to 75 per cent of men's wages. Contributing factors include the fact that women are more likely to be wage workers and unpaid family workers; that women are more likely to engage in low-productivity activities and to work in the informal sector, with less mobility to the formal sector than men; the view of women as economic dependents; and the likelihood that women are in unorganized sectors or not represented in unions.

It is calculated that women could increase their income globally by up to 76 per cent if the employment participation gap and the wage gap between women and men were closed. This is calculated to have a global value of USD 17 trillion.

Women bear disproportionate responsibility for unpaid care work. Women devote 1 to 3 hours more a day to housework than men; 2 to 10 times the amount of time a day to care (for children, elderly, and the sick), and 1 to 4 hours less a day to market activities. In the European Union for example, 25 per cent of women report care and other family and personal responsibilities as the reason for not being in the labour force, versus only three per cent of men. This directly and negatively impacts women's participation in the labour force.

Gender inequalities in time use are still large and persistent in all countries. When paid and unpaid work are combined, women in developing countries work more than men, with less time for education, leisure, political participation and self-care. Despite some improvements over the last 50 years, in virtually every country, men spend more time on leisure each day while women spend more time doing unpaid housework.

Women are more likely than men to work in informal employment. In South Asia, over 80 per cent of women in non-agricultural jobs are in informal employment, in sub-Saharan Africa, 74 per cent, and in Latin America and the Caribbean, 54 per cent. In rural areas, many women derive their livelihoods from small-scale farming, almost always informal and often unpaid .

More women than men work in vulnerable, low-paid, or undervalued jobs. As of 2013, 49.1 per cent of the world's working women were in vulnerable employment, often unprotected by labour legislation, compared to 46.9 per cent of men. Women were far more likely than men to be in vulnerable employment in East Asia (50.3 per cent versus 42.3 per cent), South-East Asia and the Pacific (63.1 per cent versus 56 per cent), South Asia (80.9 per cent versus 74.4 per cent), North Africa (54.7 per cent versus 30.2 per cent), the Middle East (33.2 per cent versus 23.7 per cent) and Sub-Saharan Africa (nearly 85.5 per cent versus 70.5 per cent).

Gender differences in laws affect both developing and developed economies, and women in all regions. Almost 90 per cent of 143 economies studied have at least one legal difference restricting women's economic opportunities. Of those, 79 economies have laws that restrict the types of jobs that women can do. And husbands can object to their wives working and prevent them from accepting jobs in 15 economies.

Women's economic equality is good for business. Companies greatly benefit from increasing leadership opportunities for women, which is shown to increase organizational effectiveness. It is estimated that companies with three or more women in senior management functions score higher in all dimensions of organizational effectiveness.

Ethnicity and gender interact to create especially large pay gaps for minority women. In 2013 in the US for instance, "women of all major racial and ethnic groups earn less than men of the same group, and also earn less than white men…Hispanic women's median earnings were USD 541 per week of full-time work, only 61.2 per cent of white men's median weekly earnings, but 91.1 per cent of the median weekly earnings of Hispanic men (because Hispanic men also have low earnings). The median weekly earnings of black women were USD 606, only 68.6 per cent of white men's earnings, but 91.3 per cent of black men's median weekly earnings, which are also fairly low. Earnings for a full-time week of work leave Hispanic women well below, and Hispanic men and black women not much above, the qualifying income threshold for receipt of food stamps of USD 588.75 for a family of four".

## Essential to agriculture

- Women comprise an average of 43 per cent of the agricultural labour force in developing countries, varying considerably across regions from 20 per cent or less in Latin America to 50 per cent or more in parts of Asia and Africa. Despite the regional and sub-regional variation, women make an essential contribution to agriculture across the developing world.

- Women farmers control less land than do men, and also have limited access to inputs, seeds, credits, and extension services. Less than 20 per cent of landholders are women.

Gender differences in access to land and credit affect the relative ability of female and male farmers and entrepreneurs to invest, operate to scale, and benefit from new economic opportunities.

• Women are responsible for household food preparation in 85-90 per cent of cases surveyed in a wide range of countries.

## The green economy, sustainable development

• From 1990 to 2010, more than 2 billion people gained access to safe drinking water, but 748 million people are still without clean drinking water.

• Women, especially those in poverty, appear more vulnerable in the face of natural disasters. A recent study of 141 countries found that more women than men die from natural hazards. Where the socioeconomic status of women is high, men and women die in roughly equal numbers during and after natural disasters, whereas more women than men die (or die at a younger age) where the socioeconomic status of women is low. Women and children are more likely to die than men during disasters.

• Women and children bear the main negative impacts of fuel and water collection and transport, with women in many developing countries spending from 1 to 4 hours a day collecting biomass for fuel. A study of time and water poverty in 25 sub-Saharan African countries estimated that women spend at least 16 million hours a day collecting drinking water; men spend 6 million hours; and children, 4 million hours . Gender gaps in domestic and household work, including time spent obtaining water and fuel and processing food, are intensified in contexts of economic crisis, environmental degradation, natural disasters, and inadequate infrastructure and services.

## A case study

Without timely help from local police officers, Purity Soinato Oiyie, a 22-year-old Maasai woman from Kenya, would have been genitally circumcised as a child, then married off to a 70-year-old man, the Commission on the Status of Women heard at the opening of its sixty-second session.

Instead, she became the first woman in her community to finish university and now she dreams of pursuing a graduate degree, Ms. Soinato Oiyie told the Commission, whose session focused on the priority theme of achieving gender equality and the empowerment of rural women and girls. Wearing a Maasai necklace beaded with the words "Stop FGM" [female genital mutilation], she delivered a joint statement on behalf of civil society, with Tarcila Rivera Zea, a Quechuan activist in Peru and leader in the indigenous women's movement. Ms. Rivera Zea said that, while previous generations had aimed at female literacy, new dreams, such as those of Ms. Soinato Oiyie, were now building ever brighter futures.

**Soroptimists**

What could happen if women of
faith built each other up?
We are more powerful together
than divided.

# Chapter VII
# Some NGOs that participated in CSW62

*We build alliances among indigenous women: at local, regional, even global levels. "Their diversity should be recognized."*
*They are "under-represented in the public domain." ...*
*"We need solidarity and recognition from other countries."*
— Chanda Thapa

## The Role of NGOs

- It can run balsanskar Kendra (Child Care Centre), Anganwadi (shelter for mother and child) and day care centers for the children of the women working in farms far away from their homes or as labours.

- It can hone the traditional skills of the rural women and by the mean of technical mediums/training facilitate mass production. Also by organizing workshops and training sessions for design and requirements to update their traditional skills and to elevate them to global standards of production.

- The foremost responsibility of any NGO is to work in the direction of social awareness. For this, it should reach out to small women groups, know about their problems through interface, and then effectively work to resolve them. In other words, an NGO should aim to satisfy local needs.

- The primary necessity of the entire world is food and milk. Under this situation, an NGO can form women farmers' organizations or clubs and provide them intense training for increasing the production of food grain and about how to take more crop depending on the seasonal cycles among the others. Especially, it should focus on milk producing groups. The rural women should be trained for how to form such group, how to maintain the accounts etc.

- The Central and State Government have taken up projects to form Women Self Help Groups. An NGO should take initiative to help such groups to work effectively.

- The major scope for any NGO is in the area of skill development

"It can also disseminate information about literacy programmes and health oriented programmes. In order to break the vicious cycle of challenges we need to focus on their strength and create new opportunities to convert the challenges into opportunities. After winning their confidence, it becomes easy to convince them to participate in programmes. Our team focused to conduct programmes that helped to get 'solution/s through economic empowerment.' We offered them three tier models here," says Dr Bhavna Joshipura of Bhavnagar, India.

1. Counseling and training

2. Creating Self Help Group

3. Literacy

## Organisers: NGO Committee on the Status of Women

The NGO Committee on the Status of Women, New York (NGO/CSW/NY) is one of three women's committees of the Conference of NGOs in Consultative Relationship with the UN (CoNGO). Established in 1972, it provides an open forum for women's voices to be heard at the United Nations. The NGO/

CSW/NY assists girls and women of all ages to advocate and organize for the implementation of global agreements, including the Nairobi Forward Looking Strategies, Beijing Platform for Action, UN Security Council Resolution 1325 (among others), the Millennium Development Goals and the Convention on the Elimination of All Forms of Discrimination against Women (CEDAW). The committee works in cooperation with the NGO Committees on the Status of Women in Geneva and Vienna.

The purpose of the NGO Committee on the Status of Women at the United Nations Headquarters in New York is:

1. To provide a forum for the exchange of information and for substantive discussion on issues and policies related to women under UN consideration and other relevant women-related studies and programs;

2. To assist the international community in implementing the Nairobi Forward-looking Strategies and the Beijing Platform for Action and decisions reached at subsequent major United Nations conferences as they relate to the advancement of women;

3. To facilitate cooperation among its member organizations, in areas of mutual interest, in the exercise of the consultative function and in activities supportive of women-related United Nations objectives;

4. To continue to work with the United Nations and its Commission on the Status of Women, the Division for the Advancement of Women, and other appropriate bodies and agencies within the United Nations system.

5. To work to mainstream a gender perspective throughout the UN system.

• Committee membership includes almost 200 national and international non-governmental organizations and individuals who promote the status of women internationally by working at local, national and international levels on the issues addressed by the United Nations. NGO/CSW/NY represents more than 80 member organizations that are concerned about the status of women and active at the UN headquarters in New York. Voting members are those individuals who represent organizations in Consultative Status with the UN through the Economic and Social Council (ECOSOC); there is one vote per organization. Individuals may be members without vote.

- Members receive notices of monthly meetings, special publications and updates on activities of the UN, plus invitations to all special events, receptions and meetings sponsored by the NGO/CSW/NY. In addition, the NGO/CSW/NY brings NGO representatives together to issue joint statements, facilitates NGO participation at CSW meetings, conducts training and orientation for NGO representatives, and runs an international listserv that keeps women worldwide apprised of issues throughout the world.

- At meetings of the Economic and Social Council, the United Nations General Assembly, the Commission on Population and Development, as well as the Commissions on Social and Sustainable Development, the NGO/CSW/NY facilitates interaction between multiple stakeholders, including women's NGOs, the UN, governments, and the private sector. In collaboration with sister committees in Geneva and Vienna, the NGO/CSW/NY organizes the NGO Consultation Day in preparation for the UN Commission on the Status of Women (CSW) meetings. It convenes morning briefings at the UN, thematic and regional caucuses, and NGO parallel events during the annual CSW meetings.

- The NGO/CSW/NY also works in partnership with other CoNGO committees to inform the UN and UN Women on a wide range of issues including violence against women,

women's health, migrant and refugee women, indigenous people's rights, and the environment.

- The annual calendar of activities for the NGO/CSW/NY includes the NGO Consultation followed by ten days of NGO activities during the CSW; a luncheon to honor CEDAW experts; a Woman Ambassadors' Luncheon at which awards are presented to new women ambassadors; presentation of a Woman of Distinction Award for an outstanding woman leader from a developing country; a Roundtable briefing to prepare for the CSW (jointly sponsored with UN Women); joint events with ECOSOC related to priority themes for the ECOSOC Annual Ministerial Review; and panel discussions for members concerning current issues at the UN via monthly meetings.

- **There were many NGOs who participated in the UN CSW 62in March this year. Here are some details of some of the NGOs who sent delegates to speak at the convention**

## The National Democratic Institute

The National Democratic Institute, or National Democratic Institute for International Affairs, is a non-partisan, non-profit NGO that works with partners in developing countries to increase the effectiveness of democratic institutions. Founded in 1983 by Madeleine Albright it is based in Washington and the President is Kenneth D Wollack.

NDI's core program areas include citizen participation, elections, debates, democratic governance, democracy and technology, political inclusion of marginalized groups, and gender, women and democracy. The organization's stated mission is to "support and strengthen democratic institutions worldwide through citizen participation, openness and accountability in government.

In 30 years, the National Democratic Institute has worked in 132 countries and territories around the world and supported the efforts of 15,000 civic organizations, 850 political parties and organizations, 10,000 legislators, and 1,300 women's organizations. Furthermore, NDI has organized over 150 international election observer delegations in over 62 countries. NDI has monitored over 340 referenda and elections and trained over 3 million election observers in over 85 countries. Furthermore, they have helped partner groups organize 300 candidate debates in over 35 countries

## Women's Rehabilitation Centre

**Women's Rehabilitation Centre** (WOREC) Nepal works in partnership with grassroots people to campaign for the promotion of human rights and sustainable community development based on social justice. Among its programmes, WOREC runs a campaign on violence against women, which includes women human rights defenders' concerns. WOREC has initiated a National Alliance of Women Human Rights Defenders in 72 districts in Nepal with the aim of developing the capacity of women human rights defenders at the community level, creating a support system for those at risk, and systematically documenting cases of violence against women human rights defenders in order to advocate with the government for effective legal mechanisms for their security and protection.

## Soroptimist International

Soroptimist International is a worldwide volunteer service organization for business and professional women who work for peace and in particular to improve the lives of women and girls, in local communities and throughout the world. Founded in 1928 its Headquarters are at Cambridge, UK.

Soroptimist means "best for women"—an organization of women at their best helping other women to be their best. As a volunteer organization of business and professional women they feel uniquely qualified to help women and girls live their dreams.

It's true that both men and women live in poverty, face discrimination and must overcome obstacles. But throughout history—in every country in the world—women and girls face additional obstacles and discrimination solely because of their gender.

- One in three women have been beaten, coerced into sex or otherwise abused in their lifetime.

- According to a recent report, of the 600,000-800,000 people trafficked across international borders annually, 80 percent are female.

- Women work two-thirds of the world's working hours but earn only 10 percent of the world's income, and own less than 1 percent of the world's property.

- Of a total 550 million working poor, 330 million (60 percent) are women.

- The United Nations estimates that globally women's unpaid care is worth up to $11 trillion annually.

- Two-thirds of the 880 million illiterate adults are women.

- Of the more than 110 million children not in school, approximately 60 percent are girls.

- By age 18, girls have received an average of 4.4 years less education than boys.

- In some countries in sub-Saharan Africa, adolescent girls have HIV rates up to five times higher than adolescent boys.

- Pregnancies and childbirth-related health problems take the lives of nearly 146,000 teenage girls each year.

- An estimated 450 million adult women in developing countries are stunted, a direct result of malnutrition in early life.

- Two million girls and women are subjected to female genital mutilation every year, and thousands suffer needlessly from obstetric fistula.

By initiating club projects that benefit women and girls, and by honoring women who help women and girls, Soroptimist clubs and members improve the status of women and girls. Soroptimist projects and programs aid women economically, and empower them to make positive changes in their lives and their communities.

Their Dream Programs empower women and girls everywhere to live their dreams. The Live Your Dream: Education and Training Awards for Women (formerly the Women's Opportunity Awards) reach more than 1,600 women a year with $1.7 million in funding. Award recipients consistently report completing or continuing their education, getting a better job, increasing their self-esteem, improving their standard of living and serving as a role model for their children. Live Your Dream Award recipients are an inspirational group of women. In addition to the funds to support their education and training, they say that being honored by an organization of women helping other women helps keep them motivated to reach their goals.

In 2015, Soroptimist launched Dream It, Be It: Career Support for Girls to provide resources to girls in secondary schools who face obstacles to their future success. The program gives girls access to professional role models, career education and resources to live their dreams. Topics covered include career opportunities, setting and achieving goals, overcoming obstacles to success, and how to move forward after setbacks or failures.

• **Zonta International**

Zonta International is an international service organization with the mission of advancing the status of women. The first Zonta Club was founded in Buffalo, New York, United States, in 1919 by a group of businesswomen under the leadership of Marian de Forest. It was organized along the lines of the Rotary Club, with one woman from each business classification admitted to the local club and all members required to give 60% of their time to the "work under which they are classified". By 1923 clubs had been established in New York City, Washington, D.C., Detroit, Cleveland, and Toledo, Ohio.

The Confederation of Zonta Clubs was formed in 1930. Originally conceived as a female equivalent of the Lions Clubs (an organization that, until 1987, was all-male), Zonta sponsors program to help women in the field of public affairs and policy making. It has consultative status with the Council of Europe, the United Nations (UN), ILO, and several UN agencies.

Currently, Zonta International is headquartered in Oak Brook, Illinois. The organization has more than 31,000 members in 65 countries. The organization's name derives from the Lakota zónta meaning "honest" or "trustworthy.

Zonta International seeks to provide opportunities for women through a number of educational programs and awards.

Amelia Earhart Fellowship: Established in 1938 in honor of famed pilot and Zontian Amelia Earhart, the Amelia Earhart Fellowship is awarded annually to women pursuing Ph.D./doctoral degrees in aerospace-related sciences or aerospace-related engineering. The Fellowship of US$10,000, awarded to 35 Fellows around the globe each year, may be used at any university or college offering accredited post-graduate courses and degrees in these fields.

## Temple of Understanding: the Road to 2020

Begun in 1960, the Temple of Understanding (TOU) is the only interfaith organization started by a woman, Juliet Hollister. It is also one of the oldest in North America. Originally the vision was to bring together religious leaders from all faiths and denominations to dialogue with one another and promote a more peaceful world. This was done initially by hosting large conferences and workshops. Gradually the focus centered on the United Nations, as a Non-Governmental Organization in Consultative Status with the UN Economic and Social Council by participating in world summit meetings, joining committees and coalitions and sponsoring programs.

In 2009 the Temple of Understanding launched a climate change initiative, focusing on the dire state of the planet's global warming and its impact on humanity. The global warming's impact on women and children in particular gave rise to a renewed concern for human rights, especially the right to water and food sovereignty.

The organization continues to be a leader in the interfaith movement, advocating for social justice through coalitions that can have an impact on peace and well- being for the planet and humanity. Our core belief in mediation through dialogue is grounded in what we see as a collective spiritual moral voice which needs to be included in all forms of decision making. Not only should women be included in all binding agreements but we believe that the prophetic voice of religions needs to be a guiding force. This is achieved not by creating 'one religion' but by working with secular and religious groups both at the UN and internationally to define the highest moral ground upon which to stand in order to bring peace and justice to all forms of government.

The Temple of Understanding also has a youth program designed to teach students interested in world affairs about the peacekeeping work of the UN. Every July we bring 18 to 20 college age students to the UN to attend committee meetings, High Level Forums and hear invited guests speak about their work. Our students give a presentation on a topic of their choice, engage in service opportunities and site visits to religious settings. This program has been running for 18 years and is one way we are able to develop youth global leadership with a moral and ethical perspective.

Ideally, the Temple of Understanding is creating a consciousness of transformation to a peaceful and sustainable world view. Advocating for policies that benefit the marginalized and poor, standing up to corruption and corporate interests that are harmful to our food production, air and water pollution and other injurious practices is a vital part of the moral voice we seek to uphold.

Ecumenical Patriarch Bartholomew of the Greek Orthodox Church and Pope Francis of the Roman Catholic Church are just a two examples of the kind of religious leadership that we admire in discernably standing up for humanity against the forces of greed and anti-democratic practices.

By networking with committees of other religiously oriented groups, we have been able to be an effective voice at the UN and elsewhere, to promote policies of justice, sustainability and interfaith cooperation.

– Alison Van Dyk, President of Temple of Understanding.

**Veena, Darchy, Grove and Laxmi**

## All India Shah Behram Baug Society

The All India Behram Baug Society an NGO in Consultative status with the UN ECOSOC was registered on June 3, 1983 in Delhi. Dr S C Shukla played a pivotal role in the registration. The

Zoroashtrian college building was started on October 2,1987 in Sanjan on the Maharashtra Gujarat state border and is owned by AISBBS.

The ESOSOC status was conferred in July 2004 in recognition of its global work for the upliftment of humanity by supporting the United Nations Millenium Goals for sustainable development. The Society encourages scientific and educational research. The President is Dr Meher Master-Moos, Vice President Ganesha Bejan Daruwala, and Treasurer Dr Dara Rupa. Laxmi Shah is the permanent Representative in New York for all activities.

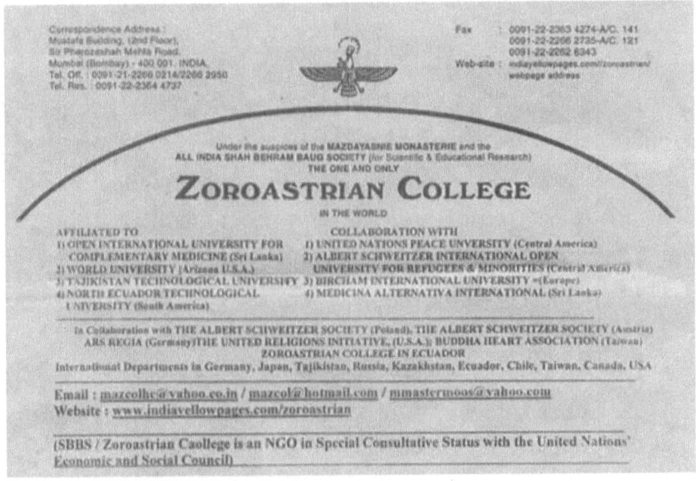

Correspondence Address :
Mustafa Building, (2nd Floor),
Sir Pherozeshah Mehta Road,
Mumbai (Bombay) - 400 001. INDIA.
Tel. Off. : 0091-21-2266 0214/2266 2950
Tel. Res. : 0091-22-2364 4737

Fax : 0091-22-2363 4274-A/C. 141
0091-22-2266 2735-A/C. 121
0091-22-2262 6343
Web-site : indiayellowpages.com/zoroastrian/
webpage address

Under the auspices of the MAZDAYASNIE MONASTERIE and the
ALL INDIA SHAH BEHRAM BAUG SOCIETY (for Scientific & Educational Research)
THE ONE AND ONLY

**ZOROASTRIAN COLLEGE**

IN THE WORLD

AFFILIATED TO
1) OPEN INTERNATIONAL UNIVERSITY FOR COMPLEMENTARY MEDICINE (Sri Lanka)
2) WORLD UNIVERSITY (Arizona U.S.A.)
3) TAJIKISTAN TECHNOLOGICAL UNIVERSITY
4) NORTH ECUADOR TECHNOLOGICAL UNIVERSITY (South America)

COLLABORATION WITH
1) UNITED NATIONS PEACE UNVERSITY (Central America)
2) ALBERT SCHWEITZER INTERNATIONAL OPEN UNIVERSITY FOR REFUGEES & MINORITIES (Central America)
3) BIRCHAM INTERNATIONAL UNIVERSITY (Europe)
4) MEDICINA ALTERNATIVA INTERNATIONAL (Sri Lanka)

In Collaboration with THE ALBERT SCHWEITZER SOCIETY (Poland), THE ALBERT SCHWEITZER SOCIETY (Austria)
ARS REGIA (Germany)THE UNITED RELIGIONS INITIATIVE, (U.S.A.); BUDDHA HEART ASSOCIATION (Taiwan)
ZOROASTRIAN COLLEGE IN ECUADOR
International Departments in Germany, Japan, Tajikistan, Russia, Kazakhstan, Ecuador, Chile, Taiwan, Canada, USA

Email : mazcolhc@yahoo.co.in / mazcol@hotmail.com / mmastermoos@yahoo.com
Website : www.indiayellowpages.com/zoroastrian

(SBBS / Zoroastrian Caollege is an NGO in Special Consultative Status with the United Nations' Economic and Social Council)

## Uganda Women's Network

The Uganda Women's Network (UWONET) is a Ugandan non-governmental organization (NGO) working to advance public policy regarding women's rights. It is an umbrella organisation of national women's NGOs and individuals operating in East Africa. The executive director is Rita H. Aciro-Lakor

During the early part of the twenty-first century, women in East Africa provided 85 percent of the agricultural work, yet owned only 7 percent of the land. Many women's rights organizations and individuals, disillusioned by groups that were not bringing women into the political process, started turning to UWONET – especially their campaign for land reform, which started in 1995. UWONET, in conjunction with the Uganda Land Alliance, lobbied Parliament in 1998 about women's right to inherit land in Uganda. In 1998, the Land Act was passed with provisions for women's rights. This campaign set a precedent for women in Uganda to "work together and to respond to issues in a more timely and aggressive way.

In 2015, UWONET, together with other organisations under The Women's Democracy Group, launched a political document, "The Women's Manifesto 2016–2021", which set out demands taken from a cross section of women in both rural and urban areas. Among other things, the document made five major demands: the betterment of women's health, land and property rights, education, economic empowerment, and decision-making in politics.

## YWCA Canada

YWCA Canada is the country's oldest largest women's multi-service organization. YWCA works in 300 communities across Canada, with Turning Point Programs for Women - which address personal safety, economic security and well-being – reach out to over 400,000 women and girls in nine provinces and two territories. YWCA is the largest national provider of shelter to women, serving 25,000 women, children and teen girls including 6,000 fleeing domestic violence each year. They are the largest provider of literacy, life skills, employment and counselling programs in the country, and the second largest provider of childcare services. YWCA Canada is a member association of the World YWCA which unites 25 million women and girls worldwide and spans 125 countries.

YWCA Canada's informed advocacy aims to:

- End violence against women and girls

- Implement national child care

- Achieve economic equality

- End homelessness for women and girls

## Tzu Chi Foundation

Buddhist Compassion Relief Tzu Chi Foundation, Republic of China, known for short as the Tzu Chi Foundation (Chinese: 慈濟基金會; literally "Compassionate Relief"), is a Taiwanese international humanitarian and non-governmental organization (NGO) with over 10 million members worldwide throughout 47 countries. It is operated by a worldwide network of volunteers and employees and has been awarded a special consultative status at the United Nations Economic and Social Council. Tzu Chi is the largest Buddhist organization in Taiwan.

The Tzu Chi Foundation was founded by Master Cheng Yen, a Taiwanese Buddhist nun, or Bhikkhuni, in 1966 as a Buddhist humanitarian organization. The foundation has several sub-organizations such as the Tzu Chi International Medical Association (TIMA) and also the Tzu Chi Collegiate Youth Association (Tzu Ching) (慈濟大專青年聯誼會 (慈青)), Tzu Chi volunteers and relief workers are mostly recognizable worldwide by their blue and white uniforms called, in Chinese: 藍天白雲, lántiān báiyún, ( lit. 'blue sky, white clouds'). The foundation's work includes medical aid, disaster relief, and environmental work such as recycling.

# GROOTS

GROOTS is a national movement of grassroots women-led community-based groups (CBOs) and Self Help Groups (SHGs) in Kenya. GROOTS Kenya has invested in nearly 2,500 women-led groups across 14 counties out of the 47 where they have direct presence. Founded in 1995 after the fourth UN Conference on Women in Beijing, China, GROOTS Kenya began as a response to the lack of visibility of grassroots women in development processes and decision-making forums that affect them and their communities.

The efforts of GROOTS Kenya have resulted in the recognition of many grassroots women as change agents at the local, national, regional and international levels winning the confidence of various partners and key stakeholders. The organization has remained committed to the bottom-up and human rights based approach to development. GROOTS Kenya works closely with communities and the administrative authorities to directly influence development processes at the county, national, regional and international levels.

GROOTS Kenya's vision is an equitable and empowered society in which women are effectively engaged in development. It is a national movement of grassroots women led community based groups (CBOs) and Self Help groups (SHGs) in Kenya.

Their theory of change is to shift grassroots women perceived role of vulnerable, victim and passive participants in development to empowered and effective leaders and agents of change in their communities.

# Bangladesh Mahila Parishad

Bangladesh Mahila Parishad (BMP, Women's Council of Bangladesh) is a women's human rights organization that was established on 4 April 1970. After the liberation war, Bangladesh Mahila Parishad was registered under the society act in 1976, in the free Bangladesh. It is supported by <u>Norway</u>.

- Bangladesh Mahila Parishad (BMP) is a voluntary membership based national action oriented mass women's organization working since 1970.

- For gender equality BMP focuses on activity concerning empowerment of women by enjoying their equal rights & dignity in the family, society and state.

- BMP is pioneering the movement of resisting violence against women political empowerment and establishment of Constitutional Rights of women since inception.

- BMP is working in the light of Convention on the Elimination of All Forms of Discrimination (CEDAW), the Convention on the Rights of Children (CRC), Human Rights Declaration, Cairo Declaration and Beijing Platform for action (BPFA).

- Besides gender issue BMP also laid emphasis on promoting peace and democracy to establish equity based society having good Governance.

- Number of General Member's: More than 0.135 million.

- Area of operation: 61 District branches within country around 2278 local units at grassroots level.

- Membership Criteria: Women aged 16 years or above belonging to any status, occupation, religion, having commitment to Women's emancipation and committed to avoid the constitution of organization are eligible for membership.

**Vision**

- Establish Secular, Democratic, Equity based Human Society and state.

**Goal**

- Women's emancipation through empowerment.

## Ventura County Women's Forum

The Ventura County Women's Forum Collaborative is a non-profit organization dedicated to empowering Ventura County women around the 12 critical areas of concern including the economy, environment, girl-child, violence, media, education, institutional mechanisms for advancement, peace, human rights, poverty, power sharing and health.

## Apne Aap Women Worldwide (India)

Apne Aap Women Worldwide is a registered charitable trust in India. A grassroots Indian organization, they work to empower girls and women to resist and end sex trafficking by organizing marginalized women and girls into small self-empowerment groups, where they work collectively to access their legal, social, economic, and political rights. <u>Founded by twenty-two courageous women in prostitution</u>, who had a vision for a world where no woman could be bought or sold, Apne Aap Women Worldwide is determined to make their vision a reality.

## Apne Aap International (US)

Based in New York, Apne Aap's international office fundraises to support its grassroots work in India. It also partners with other organizations, including the NoVo Foundation, Coalition Against Trafficking in Women, and Equality Now, to demand an end to sex trafficking.

Apne Aap helps marginalized women and girls work collectively to lift themselves out of the sex industry as well as to advocate for policy change to stem the demand for purchased sex. Since 2002, they have formed 150 self-empowerment groups in brothels, red light districts, slums, and villages. They have created and proven a community-centered solution to end sex trafficking; helped to transform the most marginalized girls and women into leaders who can change their own fates and those of their peers.

On the policy side, they successfully lobbied for the United Nation's anti-trafficking fund for survivors. Established in 2001, the fund disburses grants to organizations working at the forefront of providing services to trafficking victims. Representatives from Apne Aap have also made speeches to the South African and Icelandic parliament, urging them to change how their laws address the demand for trafficking. Today, both countries have changed their policies so that they punish buyers instead of trafficked women.

Apne Aap stands for a Third Way of dealing with sex trafficking and prostitution. They want girls and women trapped in prostitution to be decriminalized, which means they should not be punished by the law for being in prostitution or having to conduct any ancillary activities connected to prostitution like soliciting. For most women, prostitution is a survival strategy at best and bonded labor and slavery at worst. Most women and girls are forced into prostitution by circumstances or actual physical brutality. Prostitution is not a choice but results from the absence of choice since most women who are forced into prostitution come from marginalized castes, classes, races, religions, and ethnicities.

Ruchira Gupta is a journalist, social justice activist, feminist campaigner, visiting professor at New York University, Distinguished Scholar at University of California-Berkeley, and founder-president of Indian anti-sex-trafficking organization, Apne Aap Women Worldwide, which serves more than 20,000 at risk and prostituted girls and women and their family members. She has pioneered gender-sensitive interventions to end inter-generational prostitution among De-Notified Tribes in Bihar, Delhi, Haryana, Rajasthan and West Bengal.

## Rural Women New Zealand

"Women and children living in rural New Zealand have particular challenges and can be vulnerable to physical and psychological abuse due to their geographic and social isolation. For some, living rurally means they are some distance from their families and whānau and do not have the support that the wider family can provide. Family violence victims in rural New Zealand do not have the same level of access to psychological and legal support as urban women and children do, due to living rurally.

"RWNZ hope that this boost announced by the Government will be used to empower our rural communities by giving women and children who are victims of violence the help and support they so badly need," says Ms Mudford.

## International Alliance of Women

Founded in 1904 and based in Geneva, the International Alliance of Women (IAW) is an international NGO comprising 41 member organizations involved in the promotion of the human rights of women and girls globally. The IAW has general consultative status with the UN Economic and Social Council and is accredited to many specialized UN agencies, has participatory status with the Council of Europe and is represented at the Arab League, the African Union and other international organizations.

## Utah Valley University

A Utah Valley University (UVU) delegation, comprised of 26 members, participated at the 62nd session of the Commission on the Status of Women (CSW62)

One of the goals of the visit of UVU delegation was to raise awareness at the CSW62 about the lack of attention to the mountain women globally, who are among the poorest and vulnerable to such challenges as climate change and outmigration. As one of the initiatives to address it, UVU delegation presented a student engaged learning (SEL) model to advocate the implementation in the State of Utah of the sustainable development goal (SDG) #5 in interaction with mountain targets by hosting the international

Women of the Mountains conferences (WOMC) since 2007. The UVU SEL model provides students an opportunity to gain experiences and professional skills as a group through hands-on activities with faculty serving them as mentors with the UIMF representing its core.

# Chapter VIII
# Indian Women speakers at CSW62

*We must get out of our silos and recognize interdependence. Every man and woman should become involved... Local and indigenous knowledge can benefit us all, help lead to improved environmental outcomes.*
— Mary Robinson

## Ruchira Gupta

Founder of Apne Aap NGO, Ruchira Gupta is a 32-year who has campaigned relentlessly for a world in which no girl or woman is bought or sold. Among her distinctions are the French Chevalier of the Légion d'honneur, the Litterarum Humaniorum Doctors, Smith College, the Clinton Global Citizen award, Sera Bangali and the Emmy for her documentary, *The Selling of Innocents,* on the trafficking of children from Nepal to Mumbai.

She led survivors after the 16 Dec bus rape to testify to the Verma Commission and to leaders of political parties in India's Parliament for the passage of the Indian anti-trafficking law, Section 370 I.P.C, as part of the Criminal Law Amendment Act, 2013.

She participated actively in discussions that led to the passage of the UN Protocol to end Human Trafficking, Especially Women and Children, testified to the US Senate for the passage of the first US Trafficking Victim Protection Act, has spoken in the French

Assembly, Icelandic Parliament, South African Parliament, and Indian Parliament for survivor-friendly laws. By taking survivors to speak with her at the UN General Assembly and to the Human Rights Council in Geneva, she has successfully advocated for the creation of the Trafficking Fund for Survivors at the United Nations Office for Drugs and Crime.

She contributed to the creation of the National Plan of Action against trafficking in Kosovo and the SG's Zero Tolerance Policy against Sexual Violence. She has worked with UNAIDS, WHO, UN, UNIFEM and UNICEF in Nepal, Thailand, Kosovo, New York, Washington DC and Iran.

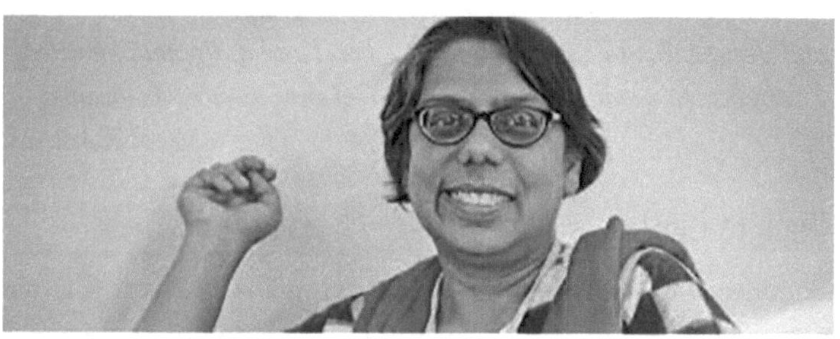

## Dr. Bhavna Kamlesh Joshipura

Dr. Bhavna Kamlesh Joshipura is a senior advocate by profession. After graduating from the science stream with physics as her major subject, she did her Masters in law. She has also studied journalism, Human Rights and International Humanitarian Law. She has done her doctoral research on 'The Social Impact of Women Empowerment - A Legal Study'. She was born in a town called Surendranagar and from childhood had shown qualities of diligence, articulation and leadership. She was the first lady president of Surendranagar Bar Association, first lady home guard officer of her town and was the lady to get elected as an independent candidate in municipality of Surendranagar and had acted as chairperson in many committees.

To fight for the case of suspect death of a woman, cases of harassment of the fair sex, without getting influenced by any bigwigs or stalwarts, going deep into the investigation is her innate nature. From her early days, she was involved in the rehabilitation of the prisoners, helping to locate the missing children and help them to get back home, rehabilitating the misguided children and fighting for the issues of child and women victimization and was looked upon as a steadfast champion of the exploited. Many children and women owe their happy life to her constant efforts.

With a *mantra* of "Self Sufficient Woman, Happy Family" she started a self-employment centre and is working for the awareness and empowerment of the women. In the field of social awareness of women, she was conferred the Vivekanand Award, the highest award of the State and The Governor Award among the others. She provides free legal advice and help at various levels to the women in distress and dire need.

She was the first lady mayor of Rajkot Municipal Corporation. Many projects in almost all the backward areas of Rajkot city and rural areas around the city are carried out under her able guidance. She has provided a strong leadership in the social issues like campaigns for 'Save the Girl Child', 'Awareness Against Malnutrition' or 'NIrbhaya cases' (cases of rape).

## Dr Pam Rajput

Pam Rajput, is an Indian academic turned internationally renowned activist who has been engaged in the women's movement since the mid-70s both in India and internationally. She helped organize and was the first Speaker of a "Women's Parliament" that brought together over 500 women leaders from every part of India. A recipient of many academic fellowships, she is a member of several expert committees and bodies in India including the nation's: Planning Commission, Ministry of Women & Child Development, National Commission for Women, delegation to the UN Commission on the Status of Women, and many others. She is also the founder and Director of the Centre for Women's Studies & Development and the Head of the Department of Political Science at Panjab University.

## Dr Nandini Azad

Dr. Nandini Azad is the vice chairperson of the ICA-AP committee on Women. Chairperson of The Independent Commission for People's Rights and Development, New Delhi; President ,India Co-operative Network for Women Limited, Board Member of National Women's Credit Fund , Acting Chairperson, Women's Committee International Co-operative Alliance, Asia-Pacific and many others. She is also the author of the Second data study.

"Social change is coming through the work of the Indian Cooperative Network for Women which is one of the few that addresses both violence against women and financial inclusion", says Dr. Azad.

## Dr Veena Adige

Dr Veena Adige is a journalist and an educator. She is the author of four books and six ebooks. She was instrumental in starting The Hitavada Twinkle Club in Nagpur which has over 25,000 children as members and is in the Limca Book of Records. Dr Adige is the Joint Secretary of Bharatiya Vidya Bhavan, Navi Mumbai Kendra. She started Vsisters, a democratic group of housewives in which the latent talent of each member is tapped and helped to reach the highest level. She and her husband are keenly interested in a rural school in Panvel, near Mumbai which has 440 students now (from 8 when they started) and has students from the nearby seven villages. The first batch of students appeared for the SSC Board exam in 2018 and secured a cent per cent result.

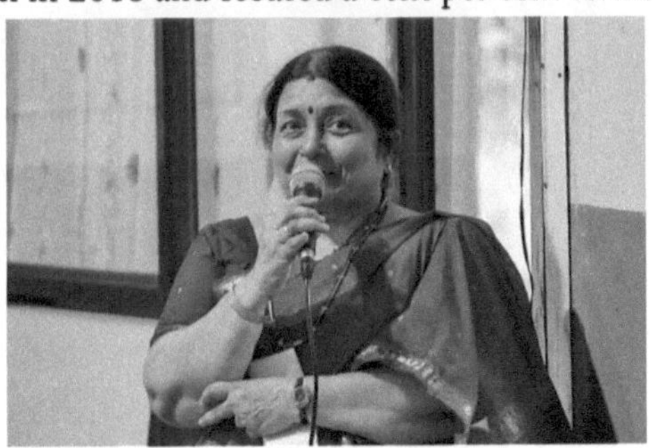

# Chapter IX
## Cultural Events

There were quite a few cultural events hosted by different countries for the delegates. There was a good response and the people enjoyed them. Here are a few ones:

International Day of Happiness (March 20) saw the Kingdom of Bhutan present a special art exhibit on happiness with a series of paintings, and UNA-USA's own delegate Rolanda Smalls engaged the world (and UN Security!) with Free Warm Hugs signage just outside the UN building. I joined her and we met (and hugged) people from all across the world, including Kazakhstan, Mali, South Africa, Iran and New York City!

There were loads of special events on World Water Day (March 22), including the launch of the International Decade of Water in the General Assembly Hall with a high level luncheon earlier in the day. To me, the clear favorite at the UN was the evening's light show hosted by the Kingdom of the Netherlands: Waterlicht. This light show was held outside, along the East River and attended by hundreds of people. Fog machines sprayed mist into the air and blue-light was cast upon water droplets, giving you the feel of being underwater. The purpose of Waterlicht was to help participants understand the impact of floods and climate change. For centuries, The Netherlands' Waterlicht outdoor light show on World Water Day, with ocean-like clouds covering UN grounds. Holland has been the leading innovator in flood management for as long as canals and flood management have been around...

The Kingdom of Bahrain hosted the Global Award for Women's Empowerment in the Delegates Dining Room, a new annual award of Princess Sabeeka bint Ibrahim Al Khalifa honoring global rockstar women making an impact for equality. Tasty treats were served alongside a sweet ceremony attended by the E.D. of UN Women, Phumzile Mlambo-Ngcuka, who appeared the busiest and most sought-after person during the entirety of CSW62. Yes, perhaps more so than the Secretary General himself!

Of course, the UN Book and Gift stores boast some remarkable authors' books and artisanal, sustainable crafts. Though for a truly special, hand-designed gift, you'll find Joe Haddad's Earth-Woman t-shirt, replete with laurel leaf. Joe is a decades-long volunteer at World Federation of United Nations Associations (WFUNA) gift store just across from the UN bookstore.

On March 11, the Permanent Mission of Nigeria to the UN hosted an evening of art and hope with a focus on Unity in Diversity. Spoken word, dance, song, comedy, and film connected the hundreds in attendance at the General Assembly.

# Quotable Quotes

These are quotes from some of the lady speakers at the CSW62 forum (March 2018)

- Phumzile Mlambo-Ngcuka: We need a people-centered approach. Rural women must be part of decision-making.

- Anastasia Mikova, film maker: Women don't always know how strong they are.

- Gia Gaspard Taylor, Network of Rural Women Producers: Extractive industries ignore environmental concerns.

- Ruth Faircloth, Rural Migrant Ministry: [What I am most proud of:] Making it here from my life as a farm worker.... We rural women need to stand up and say, "We are somebody." Women coming together here and all speaking together have a powerful voice. Let's not just talk about it. Let's do it.

- Maria Luisa Mendonça: Since the 2008 financial crisis there has been much investment in rural lands, causing displacement of rural populations and forcing them to migrate to cities. The plantation model of agriculture... generates violence.

- Marilou McPhedran, Canadian MP: We have good international frameworks. "It's time to go local."

- Urvashi Gandhi: Dialogue is more effective than debate. We need "conversations."

- Meesha Brown, PCI Media: Media can make change on both a micro and a macro level.

- Yeva Avakyan, Save the Children: "When there is no data, there is no accountability."

- Lyric Thompson (ICRW): Legal and policy changes occur first, but there is inadequate investment in programs.... Girls' clubs and other groups help girls to learn communication and negotiating skills. But "You can't expect girls to make all the needed changes on their own." Institutional and economic changes also are needed.

- A Sesame Street staff member: A microphone and a million views can be very empowering.

- Mercia Andrews, Rural Women's Assembly: South Africa has a "resource curse." Farmlands and biodiversity have come under attack (by extractive industries and agribusiness).

- Agnes Kirabo, Good Rights Alliance: The CSW probably has power to do more than it presently does. Our declarations on women are not at all binding. They just let us do this, so we will go home smiling.

- Debra Jones, Moderator of the March 12 Save the Children panel: Not investing [in children] actually costs a lot.

- Aili Keskitalo, Sami Parliament President, RECOGNIZING AND RESPECTING MARGINALIZED WOMEN, AND ALL WOMEN Women's history has been a kind of ""stepchild history." In Norway women got the right to vote in 1913. But men still dominated politics. Women were the first to tame reindeer.

- Joan Carling :Women actors should be at the center, not just regarded as program ""beneficiaries" or "victims." Their rights and their contributions must be recognized.

- Joline :I don't want people to look at me and pity me. I want people to know that my indigenous values and knowledge can do much for the world. ... We need to recognize the contributions of indigenous peoples, not just shed tears over their problems.

- Hanne Bjurstrom: Overcoming Pain and Building self-esteem: There is a culture of silence, a reluctance to discuss internal conflicts with outsiders. Victims face "shame and blame

- Panel Moderator: Human rights defenders deserve better protection.

- Agnes, a woman from Kenya: We have talked enough. It's time to act. Key actions are: land rights, gender responsive climate action ("Say nothing without consulting us"), and "Free, prior, and informed consent."

- Chanda Thapa: We build alliances among indigenous women: at local, regional, even global levels. "Their diversity should be recognized." They are "under-represented in the public domain." ..."We need solidarity and recognition from other countries. P(, Mar. 13)

- Pilar A. Alcala :Indigenous women are getting strength from women's movements and entering the political forum

- Violet Shivutse : We need to invest in movement-building and organizing, which enable women to join forces. They change their own lives and their communities.

- Mary Robinson: We must get out of our silos and recognize interdependence. Every kind of man and woman should become involved... Local and indigenous knowledge can benefit us all, help lead to improved environmental outcomes.

## Some of the Topics discussed during CSW62 March 2018

Land ownership rights of women, Confiscation of indigenous people's lands, Livestock rustling, Violence and other types of abuse of marginalized people, Legal recognition of indigenous groups is not always given (European Roma, N. American First Nations, Asia Indigenous Peoples Pact), Ways to seek redress violations of marginalized people's rights, Violence against human rights defenders, Ways to combat sexual and economic violence, Indigenous women in World War II (Sami), Engaging traditional leaders, Corruption Personal issues, trauma and sorrow experienced by marginalized women: need to improve self-respect, Documenting our own history, Climate change, Potential of indigenous knowledge (botany) to help solve problems, The daily water collection burden, Cooperatives, food security, Remote area people's inadequate access to transportation, Domestic violence, Importance of learning and mentorship, Indigenous people's need for solidarity and recognition from other countries, Women's need for information about laws and rights, Value of building alliances . Women' reluctance to enter politics, Media and women's access to it, Changes at the UN itself to improve gender equity and control sexual harassment besides many others.

# Abbreviations and Stats

CSW: Commission on the Status of Women

NGOs: Non Governmental Organisations

SDG: Sustainable Development Goals

CEDAW: Convention on the Elimination of All forms of Discrimination Against Women)

STEM: Science, technology, engineering and maths

Did you know that

- In 18 countries husbands can legally prevent their wives from working?

- In 39 countries, daughters and sons do not have equal inheritance rights?

- 49 countries lack laws protecting women from domestic violence?

- 19 % of women and girls aged 19 to 49 have experienced physical and/or sexual violence by an intimate partner in the past 12 months?

- Globally 750 million women and girls were married before the age of 18?

- Globally only 27% of top management jobs in media are held by women?

- Only 23% of films feature a woman protagonist?

- 21% of filmmakers are women?

# Epilogue

Today, 1.6 billion people still live in poverty, and nearly 80 per cent of the extreme poor live in rural areas. Many of them are rural women. They continue to be economically and socially disadvantaged – for instance, they have less access to economic resources and opportunities, quality education, health care, land, agricultural inputs and resources, infrastructure and technology, justice and social protection.

The outcome of the two-week meeting, known as the Agreed Conclusions adopted by Member States, puts forth concrete measures to lift rural women and girls out of poverty and to ensure their rights, well-being and resilience. These include ensuring their adequate living standards with equal access to land and productive assets, ending poverty, enhancing their food security and nutrition, decent work, infrastructure and technology, education and health, including their sexual and reproductive health and reproductive rights, and ending all forms of violence and harmful practices. Member States recognize in the conclusions rural women's important role in addressing hunger and food insecurity. This strong outcome provides a roadmap on next steps that governments, civil society and women's groups can undertake to support the realization of rural women's rights and address their needs

The Executive Director of UN Women, which serves as the CSW Secretariat, Phumzile Mlambo-Ngcuka, said: "The Commission's agreement on measures to bring substantive equality to women and girls in rural areas is a vital step forward. In the Commission's two weeks of dialogue we have heard clearly from the women and girls themselves what they want: from the rights to own property, to the need for quality infrastructure, to the rights to make decisions about their own bodies and lives. Effective action to bring the changes they need will take the continued engagement of all partners, from governments to civil society. Rural women themselves must be able to speak up and be heard in all consultations, and youth delegations must be included at all levels. These agreements are made in the meeting rooms of New York but must take effect in the lives of women and girls we are here to serve."

CSW is the single largest forum for UN Member States, civil society organizations and other international actors to build consensus and commitment on policy actions on this issue. More than 4,300 representatives from over 600 civil society organizations, and 170 Member States attended this year's Commission. These figures represent a steady increase from previous year's participation showing a growing strength and unity of women's voices around the world, and showcase the potential for civil society to leverage the agreed conclusions in their mission to hold governments accountable.

www.ingramcontent.com/pod-product-compliance
Lightning Source LLC
Chambersburg PA
CBHW051454250726
48655CB00001B/401